Guidelines for Building Leadership

GUIDELINES FOR BUILDING LEADERSHIP

(In Reference to PSUs)

P. Krishna Moorthy
G. Haranath

AKANSHA PUBLISHING HOUSE
NEW DELHI-110002 (INDIA)

AKANSHA PUBLISHING HOUSE
4649-B/21, Ansari Road
Darya Ganj, New Delhi - 110 002
Ph.: 23263193 / 9811582579 / 09435116718
Telefax: 011-23263193
Email: ektabooks@yahoo.com
www.akanshapublishinghouse.com

Guidelines for Building Leadership

First Published 2010

PRINTED IN INDIA

Published by Akansha Publishing House, New Delhi and Printed at Aryan Enterprises, Delhi.

Contents

Foreword

The multiple functions of leadership have played significant, guiding, progressive, educational, development roles in multiple fields of human development right from the emergence of mankind on this planet. When we look back at ancient times in the primitive era of hunting and gathering leadership has played a significant role. All the hunters and gatherers during the primitive stage of man's evolution and development, everybody was not endowed with knowledge, skill and organizing a small hunting, gathering group to be successful in their activity. Leadership is a generic term which embraces all kinds of human activity. One may begin with the family the primary leadership was assumed by the parent or child. It is the mother and the father who guided and lead the children in their formative age. One may think of the essential ingredients of leadership. In general it comprises of knowledge, skill, foresight, interest, commitment in helping people, organizing abilities, vision in a relative sense leadership is largely selfless endeavour to mobilize, motivate, encourage, guide, nurture, provide insight, clarification of goals to be achieved. As mankind has advanced over centuries with increase of population, technological innovations and competition in multiple fields of development sources of living need for guiding the people and leading the people progressively has become a challenge to all groups of people in the fields of production and innovation. Leadership in a simple sense is learning and guiding phenomena. You can not think of any society or a group which has advanced without the guiding and propelling factor of leadership. Leadership is a phenomenal invisible and visible factor. Leadership often operates both in silent and deliberate ways. We can not think of any field or any segment of society where there is absence of leadership. Not to repeat the factor leadership functions both in subtle and manifest ways. The present book focusing on Leadership building in public sector enterprise. Though based on a case study it brings out and highlights the contributing and significant role leadership plays in every sector of development. One may consider the present publication as a model reflecting and emphasizing every element of leadership in development and progress of an organization. The authors provide quiet interesting and relevant examples and illustrations exemplifying the functions of leadership in all sectors of development. Though it is a precise and limited study on leadership in a significant way it exemplifies significant, multifarious functions and contribution of leadership. It is not an exaggeration to say the present book may be considered as a leader in guiding personnel in the field of development.

Dr. E.D. Setty
Formerly Consultant
UNESCAP, UNESCO, CEC, AIT, Bangkok, Thailand
LIPI – Indonesia, BRAC – Bangladesh
Senior Research Fellow, UNCRD, Japan
Formerly Faculty at Asian Institute of Technology, Bangkok
Dr. MCRHRD Institute of AP
Professor at Maharshi Institute of Management, Bangalore

Preface

Though there are number of studies covering leadership in several sectors both private and public enterprises, the present study focuses briefly on select dimensions of leadership. In order to understand the nuances and changes in the values pertaining to the role and functions of leadership. The present study focuses pointedly to several operational aspects and functions of leadership.

In brief the study focuses on the following aspects in respect to leadership. To begin with chapter one focuses on dimensions of leadership. Followed by chapter 2 focusing on Theories of leadership. Chapter 2 in particular expounds various theories pertaining to leadership. Chapter 3 provides a brief review of literature pertaining to the concept and functions of leadership. Since it is an indepth study, chapter 4 describes the profile of the BEML. The 5th chapter embraces reflections of leadership as perceived by the respondents, leadership styles: self-perception and leadership styles subordinates perception.

The sixth chapter summarises the findings of the study and suggestions related to promoting, encouraging effective leadership in the organization both for its development and individual professional growth.

Acknowledgements

We would like to express our profoundest thanks to Dr. E.D. Setty for his kind foreword to the book.

At the outset, it gives us very great pleasure to place on record our profuse gratitude and heart-felt thanks to our beloved and esteemed teacher Dr. K. Seshaiah, for his scholarly guidance and inspiring suggestions in completing this work.

We fail if we could not express our thanks to all the sample respondents of employees of BEML without whose valuable cooperation this endeavour could not have been successful.

We would like to thank Dr. T. Sai Rama, Principal, SITAMS, Dr. A. Kuppurajulu, Vice-Chairman, SITAMS, Mr. K. Ranganatham, Executive Vice-Chairman, SITAMS and Mr. A. Ramachandhraih Governing Council Member, SITAMS, for their support and encouragement. We thank Sri. C.Gangi Reddy Garu, Chairman, AITS, Director C.Abhishek Reddy, AITS and Principal Dr. K.Yugandhar Reddy, AITS, Hyderabad, for their encouragement to strengthen the individual capacity. Finally we would like to thank A. Rama Chandra Reddy, Vice-Chancellor, Yogi Vemana University for his encouragement of this work. Last but not least we would like to express our gratitude to Sri. M.P.Misra for publishing this book.

Dr. P.Krishna Moorthy
Dr.G. Haranath

1

Dimensions of Leadership

Leadership means many things to many people. This is due to the changing environment of leaders in different roles in different functions in different settings starting from leadership of the family to the top positions in multinational organizations. However, the essentials of leadership are the same to all leaders in all positions. Nevertheless, due to the variation in the skills required, roles played, functions performed, issues tackled and the relationships promoted, different leaders have had different perceptions of leadership. As such, several attributes have been made both for the success and failure of leadership in the form of properties and processes or traits and styles of leaders. Further, even these attributes cannot provide a totally satisfactory guidance for the success of leadership. Hence, theoreticians and practitioners of leadership have gone to the extent of developing the 'contingency approach', which emphasizes that there is 'No single best way'. The functions, roles, variables, power, influence, success, effectiveness of leaders, and leadership in general discussed by different writers, researchers and practitioners are presented in the following passages.

Meaning and Definition of Leadership

There are as many definitions of leadership as there are

scholars who have attempted to analyze and understand the concept, but there is no universally accepted definition of it.[1]

The word 'leader' stems from the root *leden* meaning 'to travel' or 'show the way'. It has been derived from the verb "to lead." This also implies "to advance," "to expel," "to stand out," to guide and govern the actions of others. A leader is a person who leads a group of followers.

The *Oxford English Dictionary* (1933) notes that the word "leader" appeared in the English language as early as 1300 A.D. However, the word "leadership" did not appear until about 1800 A.D.[2] Albeit, leadership appears to be a rather sophisticated concept, words meaning 'chief' or 'king' are the only ones found in many languages to differentiate the ruler from other members of society. A preoccupation with leadership occurred predominantly in countries with Anglo-Saxon heritage. However, leaders have always been there in all cultures throughout history and the practice and philosophy of leaders and leadership can be gleaned from well-known writings as diverse in content, philosophy, and time as the Greek classic Homer's *Iliad*, the Old and New Testaments of the *Bible*, the *Mahabharata*, the *Ramayana*, the *Bhagavatha* and the Kautilya's *Arthashastra* in India, essays of Confucius in China, Machiavelli's *The Prince* which is concerned with rules and principles for obtaining and holding power.

But, the understanding, developing, predicting and managing the behaviour of leaders is still an enigma, despite the fact there are about 33,000 articles and books have been written about so far in 20th century.

The basic question is 'what in fact constitutes leadership?' While Gore and Silander[3] have mentioned about five thousand entries on the concept of leadership, Stogdill[4] reviewed seventytwo definitions of leadership. Karmel[5] is of the opinion that it is very difficult to settle on a single definition of leadership that is general enough to accommodate these many meanings and specific enough to serve as an operationalisation of the variable. However, there is a certain underlying unity among the various conceptualizations made in this area.

Hodge and Johnson[6] are of the opinion that, "Leadership is fundamentally the ability to form and mould the attitudes and behaviour of other individuals, whether informal or formal situation and that management relates to the formal task of decision and command." Ivancevich, Szilagyi and Wallace[7], define Leadership as "the relationship between two or more people in which one attempts to influence the other toward the accomplishment of some goal or goals."

In the words of Keith Davis[8], "leadership is the ability to persuade others to seek defined objectives enthusiastically. It is the human factor that binds a group together and motivates it towards goals." In the words of Koontz O' Donnell[9], "Leadership is the ability to exert interpersonal influence by means of communication towards the achievement of a goal." Leadership is defined by Paul Hersey and K.H. Blanchard[10] as "the process of influencing group activities towards the accomplishment of goals in a given situation."

Robbins[11] defines Leadership as "the ability to influence a group towards the achievement of goals." "Leadership is the interpersonal influence exercised in a situation, and directed, through the communication process, towards attainment of a specific goal or goals" say Tannenbaum and others.[12] According to G.R. Terry,[13] "leadership is the relationship in which one person or the leader influences others to work together willingly on related tasks to attain that which the leader desires". In the words of Ivancevich, Donnelly and Gibson,[14] "Leadership is the ability to influence through communication the activities of others individually or as a group, towards the accomplishment of worthwhile, meaningful, and challenging goals."

According to James J. Cribbin,[15] Leadership is "a process of influencing a group in a particular situation at a given point of time and in a specific set of circumstances that stimulates people to strive willingly to attain organizational objectives, giving them the experience of helping attain the common objectives and satisfaction with the types of leadership provided."

According to *Management Guru*, Peter F. Drucker,[16] "Leadership is the lifting of man's visions to higher sights, the raising of a man's performance to a higher standard, the building of a man's personality beyond its normal limitations."

Different scholars have focused on multiple aspects of leadership like: the creative and directive force of morale (Munson,[17] 1981); the process by which an agent induces a subordinate to behave in a desired manner (Bennis,[18] 1959); the presence of a particular influence relationship between two or more persons (Hollander and Jullian,[19] 1969); directing and coordinating the work of group members (Fiedler,[20] 1967); an interpersonal relationship in which others comply because they want to, not because they have to (Merton,[21] 1969); transforming followers, creating visions of the goals that may be attained, and articulating for the followers the way to attain these goals (Bass,[22] 1985; Tichy and Devanna,[23] 1986); the process of influencing an organised group toward accomplishing its goals (Roach and Behling,[24] 1984); actions that focus resources to create desirable opportunities (Campbell,[25] 1991); the leaders job is to create conditions for the team to be effective (Ginnett,[26] 1996); etc. According to

Andrew[27] (1998), some view leadership as the personal relationship between the individual and the group; others as the process of striving toward common goals and values; still others, as aspects of behaviour, whether desired and in control of the individual or, alternatively, reactive and driven by forces in the environment.

The common characteristic that can be found in many of the definitions is the 'influence', exerted by the leader. That is, he tries to influence the behaviour of others in a specific direction.

Leadership and Management

Though management and leadership are seen as synonyms, however, there is a difference between these two. The emphasis of leadership is on interpersonal behaviour. It is often associated with the willing and enthusiastic behaviour of the followers. But leadership does not necessarily take place within the hierarchial structure of organization. Many people operate as leaders without their role ever being clearly established or defined. A leader often has sufficient influence to bring about longer-term changes in people's attitudes and to make changes more acceptable. Accordingly leadership can be seen primarily as an inspirational process.

Management is more usually viewed as getting things done through and with others in order to achieve stated organizational objectives. The manager may react to specific situations and be more concerned with solving short-term problems. Management is regarded as relating to people working within a structured organization and with prescribed roles. To people outside the organization, the manager might not appear in a leadership role.[28]

The following table explains the differences between leadership and management.

Table 1.1
Leadership and Management Differences

Leadership	*Management*	
Creating an Agenda	*Establishes direction:* Develops a vision and the strategies needed for its achievement	*Plans and budgets:* Establishes detailed steps and timetables for achieving needed results; allocate necessary resources
Developing a Network for Achieving the Agenda	*Involves aligning people:* Communicates direction by words and deeds to all those whose cooperation may be needed to help create teams and coalitions that understand the vision and strategies, and accepts their validity.	*Organizes and staffs:* Establishes structure for achieving the plans; staffs; delegates responsibility and authority for implementation; develops policies and procedures to guide people; creates monitoring systems
Execution	*Motivates and inspires:* Energizes people to overcome major political, bureaucratic, and resource barriers to change by satisfying basic human needs.	*Controls and solves problems:* Monitors results against plans, and then plans and organizes to close the gap.
Outcomes	*Produces change, often to a dramatic degree:* Has the potential of producing extremely useful change, such as new products desired by managers	*Produces a degree of predictability and order:* Has the potential to consistently produce key results expected by various stockholders (such as meeting deadlines for customers and paying dividends to stockholders)

Source: John P. Kotter, *A Force for Change: How Leadership Differs from Management* (New York: The Free Press, 1990); Wayne K. Kirchner, book review of "A Force for Change," *Personnel Psychology*, Autumn 1990, P.655.

According to John P. Kotter, a prominent leadership theorist, today's managers must know how to lead as well as manage. Without leading as well as managing, organizations face the threat of extinction. Kotter[29] draws the following distinctions between management and leadership:

- Management is more formal and scientific than leadership. It relies on universal skills such as planning, budgeting, and controlling. Management is an explicit set of tools and techniques, based on reasoning and testing that can be used in a variety of situations.
- Leadership, in contrast to management, involves having a vision of what the organization can become.
- Leadership requires eliciting cooperation and teamwork from a large network of people and keeping the key people in that network motivated, using every manner of persuasion.

Functions of Leadership

Many theorists of leadership have classified the several functions of a leader and attached to him many roles. Often an overlapping can be seen among the different classifications.

In order to understand the process of leadership it is necessary to analyze the functions and responsibilities of leadership. These functions require different emphases in different situations according to the nature of the groups. A leader's position in the same group may also change over a period of time. It is possible, however, to list a range of general functions which are served by the leader. A useful summary is provided by Krech[30] who has identified fourteen functions.

1. The leader, as an executive, is a top coordinator of group activities and an oversees of the execution of policies.

2. The leader, as a planner, decides the ways and means by which the group achieves its both short-term and long-term ends through proper action and proper planning.

3. The leader, as a policy-maker, establishes the group goals and policies.

4. The leader, as an expert, is a source of information and skills.

5. The leader, as a representative is the official spokesperson for the group, the representative of the group and the channel for both outgoing and incoming communications.

6. The leader, as a controller of internal relations, determines specific aspects of the group structure.

7. The leader, as purveyor of rewards and punishment, exercises controls over the group members by the power vested in him to give rewards and impose punishments.

8. The leader, as arbitrator and mediator, controls interpersonal conflict within the group.

9. The leader, as exemplar is a role model for members of the group, setting an example of what is expected.

10. The leader, as a symbol of the group, enhances the group unit by providing some kind of cognitive focus and establishing the group as a distinct entity.

11. The leader, as a substitute for individual responsibility, relieves the individual member of the group from the necessity of, and responsibility for, personal decision.

12. The leader, as an ideologist, serves as the source of beliefs, values and standards of behaviour for individual members of the group.

13. The leader, as a father figure, serves as focus for the positive emotional feelings of individual members and the object for identification and transference.

14. The leader, as a scapegoat, serves as a target for aggression and hostility of the group, accepting blame in the case of failure.

Herbert G. Hicks[31] refer to the following as the common leadership activities:

1. *Arbitrating:* Often members disagree on the best decision for an organizational matter. An effective leader often will resolve such disagreement by arbitrating on making the decision on the course of action to be taken.

2. *Suggesting:* Suggestions are often employed by an adroit leader for a long-term. Suggestion is likely to be a powerful tool in the manager's kit.

3. *Fixing objectives:* A manager often personally fixes the objectives for his organization. He must see to it that the organization has always specific and suitable objectives before it.

4. *Catalysing:* In organizations some force is required to start or accelerate their movement. A leader is expected to be a catalyser and provide such a force.

5. *Providing security:* In organizations the personal security of followers is very important. A true leader can provide a large measure of security by maintaining a positive and optimistic attitude towards them even in the face of adversities.

6. *Representing:* A leader is usually treated as the representative of his organization.
7. *Inspiring:* In organisation many persons work more productively in organizations when their leader makes them feel that the work they do is worthwhile and important.
8. *Praising:* Managers can help to satisfy the needs of their assistants and fellow employees by sincerely praising them for the work they do.

Stogdill[32] says, "Leadership is consistent with problems of human performance and interactions."

Leadership Roles

Henry Mintzberg[33] offers a number of interesting insights into the nature of managerial roles. He concludes that managers play ten different roles, which fall into three basic categories: interpersonal, informational and decisional.

Interpersonal Roles

There are three interpersonal roles inherent in the manager's job. They are roles of figurehead, leader, and liaison, which involve dealing with other people.

First, the manager is often asked to serve as a ***figurehead***—taking visitors to dinners, attending ribbon-cutting ceremonies, and the like. These activities are typically more ceremonial and symbolic than substantive.

The manager is also asked to serve as a ***leader***—hiring, training, and motivating employees. A manager who formally or informally shows his subordinates how to do things and how to perform under pressure is leading them. Finally, the manager has a ***liaison*** role to play, which often involves serving as a coordinator or link between people, groups, or organizations.

Informational Roles

The three informational roles of the manager identified by Mintzberg flow naturally from the interpersonal roles: the roles of monitor, disseminator, and spokesperson, which involve the processing of information. The process of carrying out these roles places the manager at a strategic point to gather and disseminate information. As ***monitor***, the manager actively seeks information that may be of value to the organisation. He questions his subordinates, and is receptive to unsolicited information. As disseminator of information, he transmits relevant information to others in the workplace. When the roles of *monitor* and ***disseminator*** are viewed together, the manager emerges as a vital link in the organization's chain of communication. The third informational role as spokesperson focuses on external communication. The ***spokesperson*** formally relays information to people outside the unit or outside the organisation.

Decisional roles. Mintzberg identifies four decisional roles: entrepreneur, disturbance handler, resource allocator, and negotiator. All of them primarily relate to making decisions. First, the manager has the role of ***entrepreneur***, the voluntary initiator of change. His second role as disturbance handler is initiated not by him but by other individuals or groups. The manager responds to his role as ***disturbance handler*** by handling such problems as strikes, copyright infringements, and energy shortages, etc. In his third decisional role as ***resource allocator,*** the manager decides how resources are to be distributed, and with whom he or she should work most closely. A fourth decisional role is that of ***negotiator***. In this role the manager enters into negotiations with other groups or organizations as a representative of the company.

Leadership Variables

Every group of people that performs to its total capacity has some person as its head who is skilled in the art of influencing. This seems to be a compound of at least four major components: (1) to use power effectively and responsibly; (2) to comprehend that human beings have different motivational forces at different times and in different situations; (3) to inspire; and (4) to act in a manner that will develop a climate conducive to responding to and arousing motivations.[34]

According to McGregor[35] there are at least four variables involved in leadership. They are:

(1) Characteristics of the leader; (2) the needs, attitudes and other personal characteristics of the followers; (3) the characteristics of an organization, such as its purpose, its structure and the nature of the task to be performed; and (4) the social, economic and political environment.

Power and Influence of Leadership

Leadership influence depends upon the type of power that the leader can exercise over other people in his organization. The exercise of power is a social process, which helps to explain how different people can influence the behaviour of others.

Leadership has long been considered as one of the most important factors influencing organizational performance and achievement of goals. As such, it constitutes an important aspect of managing. The ability to lead effectively is one of the keys to become an effective manager. Effective direction is not possible by managers unless they are effective leaders. The need for effective leadership would be evident if one looks into the comparative use of authority, power and influence by managers in any organization.

Power is the capacity of one party to influence other parties to act as it wants.[36] Power can influence behaviour through compliance, identification and internationalization. It is a function of ties of mutual dependence in social relationship. Power is the ability of one to control the actions of others[37]. Robbins[38] defines power as the ability to influence and control anything that is of value to others. From an organizational point of view, it can be defined as the degree of influence an individual or group has in decision-making, without being authorised by the organisation to do so. There are multiple sources of power in leadership roles.

Henry Mintzberg's[39] classic study of what managers do on the job fails to describe the influence tactics used. French and Raven[40] propose that social power is used to influence others. They state that the bases of power include reward power, coercive power, legitimate power, referent power and expertise power.

Seven influence strategies have been proposed as particularly vital for practicing leadership roles.[41] These strategies are:

i) *Reason:* Using facts and data to develop a logically sound argument;

ii) *Friendliness:* Using supportiveness; flattery and the creation of goodwill;

iii) *Coalition:* Mobilizing others in the organization;

iv) *Bargaining:* Negotiating through the use of benefits or favours;

v) *Assertiveness:* Using a direct and forceful approach;

vi) *Higher Authority:* Gaining the support of higher levels in the hierarchy to add weight to the requests; and

vii) *Sanctions:* Using rewards and punishment.

Managerial influence is exercised through persuasions, suggestions and advice with the intention of affecting the subordinates' behaviour. In the case of influence, the subordinates will have the option of either rejecting or accepting the proposition. Chester I Bernard[42] has remarked that every management comes across "a zone of influence for authority acceptance."

Success and Effectiveness of Leadership

Factors that influence leadership effectiveness include the leader's personality, past experience and expectations; the superior's expectations and behaviour; the subordinate's characteristics, expectations and behaviour; the requirements of the task; the organizational climate and policies; and the expectations and behaviour of peers.[43] These factors also influence the leader in return. The influence process is reciprocal involving leaders and group members.

The leader's personality, past experiences and expectations

The Leader's personality or past experience helps his or her leadership style. It does not mean that the style is unchangeable. It is important to note that managers who attempt to adopt a style, that is very inconsistent with their basic personality, are unlikely to use that style effectively.

The leader's expectations are another component of leadership. Evidence has shown that, for a variety of reasons, situations tend to work out the way we expect them to; this is sometimes referred to as self-fulfilling prophecy. In fact, one study found that new leaders who were told that their subordinates were low performers managed in a much more attractive manner than new leaders who were told that their subordinates were high performers.[44]

The expectations and behaviour of superiors

The leadership style that a manager's superiors approve

of is very important in determining the orientation a manager will select. For example, a superior who clearly favours a task-oriented style may cause the manager to adopt that type of leadership. A superior who favours an employee-oriented style encourages the manager to adopt a more employee-centred orientation.

One study found that the supervisors who learned new behaviours in a human relations training programme tended to give up those behaviours quickly if they were not consistent with their immediate superior's leadership style.[45]

Subordinate's characteristics, expectations and behaviour

Subordinates play a crucial role in influencing the manager's leadership style. They are, after all, the people whom that the style is supposed to affect.

The characteristics of subordinates affect the manager's leadership style in a number of ways. Highly capable employees will normally require a less directive approach. Secondly the attitude of subordinates will also be an influencing factor.

The expectations of subordinates is another factor in determining how appropriate a particular style will be. Subordinates who have had employee-centred managers in the past may expect a new manager to have a similar style. Similarly, highly skilled and motivated workers may expect the manager not to 'meddle'. The reactions of subordinates to their manager's leadership style will usually signal to him how effective his style is.

Task requirements

The nature of subordinates' job responsibilities will also affect the type of leadership style a manager will adopt.

Similarly, where much cooperation and teamwork are involved, as in new product development, employees generally prefer people-centered supervision, whereas those working in isolation prefer more task-oriented direction.

Organizational climate and policies

The 'personality' or climate of an organization influences the expectations and behaviour of the organization members. The stated policies of the organizations also affect a manager's leadership style. In organizations where climate and policies encourage strict accountability for expenses and results, managers usually supervise and control subordinates tightly.

Peer's expectations and behaviour

One's fellow managers are an important reference group. They form friendship with their colleagues in the organization, whose opinions matter to them. In addition, the attitude of the manager's peers can often affect how effectively he performs; hostile colleagues may compete aggressively for organization resources, harm the manager's reputation, and prove uncooperative in other ways. In many ways, the behaviour of managers affects and influences that of their associates.

According to Hersey and Blanchard, there is a difference between a successful leader and an effective leader. A successful leader is one who merely changes the behaviour of his followers (and not their attitudes) by using largely his positional power. On the other hand, an effective leader is one who not only changes the behaviour of his followers but also their attitudes by using largely his personal power. The result is that in the first case the change is short-lived whereas in the second case it is enduring. Thus, all successful leaders are not effective leaders. But all effective leaders are also successful leaders. Effective leadership is a function of the leader, the followers and situations.

According to Koontz and O' Donnell,[46] "leadership" can be effective only when the following principles are complied with in the area of leading as it applied to managers:

1. *The principle of Harmony of objectives:* It calls for a careful and sincere attempt on the part of the managers desirous of proving themselves as effective leaders to enable members of the organisation to see and understand that their personal goals are in harmony with enterprise objectives.

2. *The principle of maximum clarity and integrity in communications:* Managerial leading should ensure that their communication is clear, and unambiguous so as to support understanding by the individuals for enabling them to achieve and maintain the co-operation that is required to meet the enterprise goals.

3. *The principle of supplemental use of informal organization:* In order to make the communication most effective, the manager should make the best use of informal organization as a supplement to the communication channels of formal organization.

4. *The principle of motivation:* Motivation is not a simple "cause and effect" process. Hence, managers who are keen on emerging as effective leaders should make the motivational programme very effective by

   (a) carefully assessing the reward structure;

   (b) looking upon it from a situational and contingency point of view;

   (c) integrating it into the entire system of managing;

   (d) understand correctly as to what motivates their individual subordinates;

   (e) how and in what way these motivators operate; and

(f) most sincerely reflect such an understanding in carrying out their managerial actions.

Since the human society evolved over millennia pursuing ever renewing occupations for sustainance with the growth of number need for technical assistance and guidance for operational modes of diverse pursuits for livelihood mankind over centuries looked for technical and operational guidance from people who can lead them in fruitful pursuits of their livelihood. Leadership as one could see over centuries is need oriented, objective or goals specified. Leadership as a concept is not fixed and determined to a particular activity or arena and it is evergrowing social phenomenon. The basic thing in all kinds of leadership is providing knowledge, guidance and directing and fruitfully accomplishing the task pursued by an individual or a group of individuals. In one word it is a continuous and ever enriching social phenomenon for guiding and leading people to accomplish their pursuits.

REFERENCES

1. Bennis, W. G. "Leadership Theory and Administrative Behaviour: The Problem of Authority," *Administrative Science Quarterly*, Vol.4, 1959, pp. 259-269.
2. Ralph M. Stogdill, *Handbook of Leadership: A Survey of Theory and Research*, The Free Press, New York, 1974, p.7.
3. Gore, W.J. and Silander, F.S. "A Bibliographical Essay on Decision Making," *Administrative Science Quarterly*, Vol.6, 1959, pp.121-129.
4. Stogdill, R.M., *Hand Book of Leadership: A Survey of Theory and Research*, Free Press, New York, 1974, p.7.
5. Karmel, B. "Leadership: A Challenge to Traditional Research Methods and Assumptions," *Academy of Management Review*, Vol.3, 1978, pp.475-482.
6. B.J. Hodge and Johnson H.J., *Management of*

Organisational Behaviour, John Wiley and Sons, New York, 1970, p. 250.

7. Ivancevich, Szilagyi and Wallace, *Organisation Behaviour and Performance*, p.273 (Adopted from Dr. M.J. Mathew, "Organisation: Theory and Behaviour," RBSA Publishers, Jaipur, 1993, p.181)
8. Keith Davis, *Human Behaviour at Work*, Tata McGraw-Hill Company Ltd., New Delhi, 1975, p.124.
9. Koontz O' Donnell, *Management*, McGraw-Hill International Book Company, 1st Printing, New York, 1984, p.506.
10. Paul Hersey and K.H. Blanchard, *Management of Organisational Behaviour*, Engle Wood Cliffs, Prentice Hall, New Jersey, 1977.
11. Robbins, S.P., *Organisational Behaviour: Concepts and Controversies*, Engle wood cliffs, Prentice Hall, New Jersey, 1979, p.240
12. Robert Tannenbaum, R. Weschier and Fred Massarik, *Leadership and Organisation: A Behavioural ScienceAapproach*, McGraw-Hill Book Co., Inc., New York, 1961, p.24.
13. George R. Terry, *Principles of Management*, Richard, D. Irwin, Inc. Home Wood, Illinois, 1968, p.45.
14. Ivancevich, Donnelly and Gibson, *Management Principles and Functions*, Fourth edition, All India Traveller Book seller, Delhi, 1991, p.296.
15. James J. Cribbin, "Effective Managerial Leadership," American Management Association, 1972, p.9.
16. Peter Drucker, *Practice of Management*, Allied publishers, New Delhi, 1970, p.159.
17. Munson, C.E. "Style and Structure in Supervision", *Journal of Education for Social Work*, 17, 1981 pp.65-72.
18. Bennis, W.G. "Leadership Theory and Administrative Behaviour: The Problem of Authority," *Administrative Science Quarterly*, 4, 1959.

19. Hollander, E.P., and Jullian J.W., "Contemporary Trends in the Analysis of Leadership Processes," *Psychological Bulletin*, 71, 1996, pp.387-391.

20. Fiedler, F.E., *A Theory of Leadership Effectiveness*, McGraw Hill, New York, 1967.

21. Merton, R.K. "The Social Nature of Leadership," *American Journal of Nursing*, 69, 1969, pp.2614-2618.

22. Bass, B.M., *Leadership and Performance Beyond Expectations*, The Free Press, New York, 1985.

23. Tichy, N.M. and Devanna, M.A., *The Transformational Leader*, Wiley, New York, 1986.

24. Roach, C.F. and Behling, O. "Functionalism: Basis for an Alternative Approach to the Study of Leadership," in *Leadership and Managers* by J.G. Hunt (ed.), Pergamon, New York, 1984.

25. Campbell, D.P. *Campbell Leadership Index Manual*, National Computer System, 1991.

26. Ginnett, R.C. "Team Effectiveness Leadership Model: Identifying Leverage Points for Change," Proceedings of the National Leadership Institute Conference, College Park, MD: National Leadership Institute, 1996.

27. Kakabadse, Andrew, "Leadership for the Third Millennium," *Essence of Leadership*, International Thompson Publishing, 1998.

28. Hunt, J.W., *Managing People at Work*, Second Edition, McGraw-Hill, New York, 1986, p.38.

29. John P. Kotter, *A Force for Change: How Leadership Differs from Management*, The Free Press, New York, 1990; Warren Bennis, "An Invented Life: Reflections on Leadership and Change," Addison-Wesley, Reading, Mass., 1993)...

30. Krech, D., Crutchfield, R.S. and Ballachey, E.L., *Individual in Society*, McGraw-Hill, New York, 1962, pp.26-34.

31. Herbert G. Hicks and C. Roy Gullet, *The Management of Organizations*, 3rd edition, McGraw-Hill Series in Management, New York, pp.447-449.

32. Stogdill, R.M and Coons, A.E. (eds) "Leader Behaviour its Perception and Measurement," Columbus, Bureau of Business Research, Ohio State University, 1957.

33. Henry Mintzberg, *The Nature of Managerial Work*, Harper and Row, New York, 1973; J. Kenneth Graham, Jr., and William L. Mihal, "The CMD Managerial Job Analysis Inventory," Rochester Institute of Technology, Center for Management Development, Rochester, New York, 1987, pp.2-6.

34. Koontz, H. and Weihrich, H., *Management*, 9th Edition, McGraw-Hill Company, Yew York, 1989, p.438.

35. Douglas McGregor., *The Human Side of Enterprise*, McGraw–Hill International Book Company, New York, 1960, p.182.

36. Szilagyi and Wallace, "Organisational Behaviour and Performance," Richard D. Irwin, Inc. Homewood, Illinois, 1968. p.333.

37. V.S.P. Rao and P.S. Narayana, *Organisation Theory and Behaviour*, Vikas Publishing House, New Delhi, 1986, p.656.

38. S.P. Robbins, *Organisational Behaviour*, Prentice Hall Inc., Englewood Cliffs, 1979, p.263.

39. Henry Mintzberg, *The Nature of Managerial work*, Prentice Hall, Englewood Cliffs, New Jersey, 1980.

40. John R.P. French and Betram Raven, "The Basis of Social Power," in studies in Social Power. D. Cart Wright, University of Michigan Press, Ann Arbor, 1959, pp.150-167.

41. Davis Kipnis, Stuart M. Schmidt, Chris Swaffin-Smith, and Ian Wilkinson, "Pattern of Managerial Influence: Shotgun Managers, Tacicians, and By Standards," *Organisational Dynamics*, Winter 1984, pp.58-67.

42. Chester I Barnard, *The Functions of the Executive*, Harvard University Press, Cambridge, 1946, pp. 168-169.

43. Joseph Reitz, H. "Behaviour in Organizations," Rev. Ed. (Home Wood III. Irwin, 1981) and Paul Heresy and Kenneth H. Blanchard, *Management of Organizational Behaviour*, 3rd Ed. Engle Wood Cliffs, Prentice- Hall, N.J., 1977, pp.133-143.

44. George, F. Farris and Francis, G. Lim, Jr. "Effects of Performance on Leadership, Cohesiveness, Satisfaction and Subsequent Performance," *Journal of Applied Psychology*, Vol.53, No.6, December 1969, pp.490-497.

45. Fleishman, E.A. "Leadership Climate, Human Relations Training, and Supervisory Behaviour," *Personnel Psychology*, Vol.6, No.2, Summer, 1953, pp.205-222.

46. Harold Koontz and Cyril O' Donnell, *Essentials of Management*, Tata McGraw-Hill Publishing Company, New Delhi, 1978, PP.454-455.

2

Theories of Leadership

Leadership has been discussed, analysed and understood from several dimensions. The varied experiences of people involved in the process through changing times have provided different perceptions of the subject. Consequently theoreticians and practitioners have approached the subject from their own perspectives resulting in many theories of leadership. As a result leadership has come to mean different things to different people in different contexts. Though the idea of leadership has been known from times immemorial and practised, it is in the 20th century that it has been explored/ studied in depth and theorized from many angles. Economists, sociologists, psychologists, political scientists, and anthropologists and others have been investigating into the subject. Nevertheless, there has been no consensus among them regarding it except that leadership is the relationship between a leader and his followers. Whatever may be one's position in the organizational hierarchy or institutional context; he guides, directs, or influences others towards specific objectives. However, the controversy relating to leadership regarding its meaning, inputs, processes and outputs and their impact on the motivation of people, organizational performance and executive effectiveness and success, has continued with the result that search for new theories, comprehensive and adequate, too has been going on. Leadership is akin to parental guidance in respect to children. In view of what is expected in respect to individual employee or a group in an organization. Leadership if need be for the performance of activity is to guide the individual or group to go about successfully to accomplish the task entrusted to the people. This kind of leadership may relate to knowledge related to the segments in the operational system and organizational and technical means and methods to be judiciously employed to accomplish the task assigned and specified objectives to be realized.

Theories of Leadership

In simple terms, leadership is the ability to influence a group toward the achievement of a goal. It is essential to business, government and countless groups and organizations that shape the way we live, work and play.[1] The source of influence may be formal, such as that provided by virtue of his position by the manager of an organization or informal as in other social and political organizations.

Approaches to Leadership

From the voluminous literature on leadership three basic approaches can be identified to explain what makes an effective leader. The first approach seeks to find universal personality traits that leaders have and non-leaders do not have. The second approach tries to explain leadership in terms of the behaviour that a person is engaged in. Both approaches have been considered as 'false starts', because they are based on erroneous and over-simplified conceptions.[2] Thus contingency models have been evolved not only to explain the inadequacies of earlier theories but also to identify which of the situational factors is most important for leadership and to predict which leadership style will be most effective in a given situation.

In the early twentieth century with the development of the Scientific Management Movement, increasing emphasis was laid on organizational leadership. F.W. Taylor initiated time and motion studies to analyse work tasks to improve performance in every aspect of organizational functioning. The most notable function of the leader under the Scientific Management or the classical theory was to enhance organizational effectiveness, while the primary aim of the leader was to improve organizational efficiency and not individual efficiency.

In the 1930's Taylor's emphasis was drastically modified by the Human Relations Movement that was initiated by Elton Mayo and his colleagues. Mayo emphasised that for an organization to enhance its effectiveness it has to take into account human feelings, attitudes and processes involving inter-personal interaction. Therefore, in the Human Relations School, the focus of the leader was not only on the development of the organization, but also on the growth of the individuals managing such an organization.

In recent years the assumption of Human Relations Approach has been challenged by a number of researchers like McGregor, Argyris, Schein, Likert, etc., who highlight the Human Resources Approach rather than the over-simplified approach of human relations. This approach views that human beings are influenced by a set of complex and interrelated factors. These factors take into account the enormous talent, and potential that an individual brings to his work-place with him. It is a question or giving him opportunities to utilise his talent, creativity and potentials by giving him a meaningful work assignment and by adding greater responsibility, autonomy, variety, etc.

The theories of leadership can be conveniently divided into three viz., 1. Trait theory 2. Behavioural theory 3. Contingency theory.

Trait Approach to Leadership

Early studies of leadership in the 1940s and the 1950s concluded that leadership is largely a matter of personality, a function of specific traits. A successful leader not only secures the desired behaviour from his followers but succeeds in creating a sense of satisfaction among them. Leadership traits cannot be fixed with certainty for all leaders. But a leader cannot be effective unless he possesses certain basic qualities. The following are some of the studies that attempted to identify these traits:

Ordway Tead[3] has suggested ten qualities of a good leader:

1. Physical and nervous energy,
2. Sense of purpose and direction,
3. Enthusiasm,
4. Friendliness and affection,
5. Integrity,
6. Technical mastery,
7. Decisiveness,
8. Intelligence,
9. Teaching skill, and
10. Faith.

Chester I. Barnard[4] has indicated two aspects of leadership traits:

1. Commanding subordinates admiration includes outstanding qualities in respect of physique, skill, technology, perception, knowledge, memory and imagination,
2. Individual superiority in determination, persistence, endurance and courage.

Henry Fayol[5] regards the following as the qualities of a good leader:

1. Health and physical fitness,
2. Intelligence and mutual vigour,
3. Moral qualities,
4. Knowledge, and
5. Managerial ability.

George R. Terry[6] has suggested the following qualities:

1. Energy - both mental and physical
2. Emotional stability
3. Knowledge of human relations
4. Empathy
5. Objectivity
6. Personal motivation
7. Communication skills
8. Teaching ability
9. Social skills and technical competence.

Stogdill[7] identifies through research the following traits:

1. Physical characteristics such as age, appearance, height and weight;
2. Social background-education, social status and mobility;
3. Intelligence-superior judgement, decisiveness, knowledge and fluency of speech;
4. Personality-alertness, self-confidence, personal integrity, self-assurance and dominance needs;

5. Task related characteristics-high need for achievement and responsibility, initiative and a high task orientation; and
6. Social characteristics.

Keith Davis[8] lists the following as the characteristics of leadership:

a) *Intelligence:* Leaders tend to have higher intelligence than their followers.

b) *Social maturity and breadth:* Leaders have a tendency to be emotionally mature and to have a broad range of interests.

c) *Inner motivation and achievement drives:* Leaders want to accomplish things; when they achieve one goal, they seek out another. They are not primarily dependent on outside forces for their motivation.

d) *Human relations attitudes:* Leaders are able to work effectively with other persons. They respect individuals and realize that to accomplish tasks they must be considerate to others.

Leadership Skills

Some researchers have mixed the skills with the traits resulting from the development of human relations by a leader with the subordinates.

Chris Argyris[9] mentions the following characteristics of a leader:

1. The leader is constantly interacting and commanding.
2. The leader makes the organization a part of his self image.
3. The leader's personal goals, values and feeling the organizationally centred.

4. The leader handles the supervisors as individuals.
5. The leader controls the transmission of important information.
6. The leader emphasizes the present.
7. The leader sets realistic goals.

According to Harold Koontz,[10] every group of people that performs near its total capacity has some person as its head who is skilled in the art of leadership. This skill seems to be a compound of at least four major ingredients: (1) the ability to use power effectively and in a responsible manner, (2) the ability to comprehend that human beings have different motivation forces at different times and in different situations, (3) the ability to inspire followers, and (4) the ability to act in a manner that will develop a climate conducive to responding to and arousing motivations.

Katz,[11] in his classic study of managers identifies three important types of managerial skills: technical, interpersonal, and conceptual. Diagnostic skills are also prerequisites to managerial success.

Technical skills. These are the skills necessary to accomplish or understand the specific kind of work being done in an organization.

Interpersonal skills. The ability to communicate with, understand, and motivate both individuals and group.

Conceptual skills. These depend on the manager's ability to think in the abstract. Managers need the mental capacity to understand the overall workings of the organization and its environment, to grasp how all the parts of the organization fit together, and to view the organisation in a holistic manner.

Diagnostic skills. These are skills that enable a manager to visualize the most appropriate response to a situation. Successful managers have them.

Gary Yukl[12] (1981) summarising the research in the field till his times, identified following traits and skills as characteristic of successful leaders:

Traits Characteristic of Successful Leaders:

1. Adaptable to situations
2. Alert to the social environment
3. Ambitious and achievement-oriented
4. Assertive
5. Cooperative
6. Decisive
7. Dependable
8. Dominant (the desire to influence others)
9. Energetic (high activity level)
10. Persistent
11. Self-confident
12. Tolerant of stress
13. Willing to assume responsibility

Skills Characteristic of Successful Leaders:

1. Clever (intelligent)
2. Conceptually skilled
3. Creative
4. Diplomatic and tactful
5. Fluent in speaking
6. Knowledgeable about the group task
7. Organized (administrative ability)

8. Persuasive
9. Socially skilled

Michael and Dean[13] suggest a number of leadership skills critical to success in the global economy. They include the following:

1. *Cultural flexibility*. In international assignments this skill refers to cultural awareness and sensitivity. In domestic organizations the same awareness could be increasing diversity. Leaders must have the skills not only to manage but also to recognize and celebrate the value of diversity in their organizations.
2. *Communication skills*. Effective leaders must be able to communicate, in writing, orally, and nonverbally.
3. *Human resource development (HRD)* skills. Since human resources are so much a part of leadership effectiveness, that leaders must have the HRD skills of developing a learning climate, designing training programmes, transmitting information and experience, assessing results, providing career counseling, creating organizational change, and adapting learning materials.[14]
4. *Creativity*. Problem solving, innovation, and creativity provide the competitive advantage in today's global marketplace. Leaders must possess the skills to not only be creative themselves but also provide a climate that encourages creativity and assist their people to be creative.
5. *Self-management of learning*. This skill refers to the need for continuous learning of new knowledge and skills. In the times of dramatic change and chaos, leaders must undergo continuous change themselves. They must be self-learners.

An academic analysis made by Kanungo and Misra[15] noted "the prevailing conceptualizations of skills required for successful managerial performance hinders our understanding of the phenomenon". To get over this problem, Whetten and Cameron[16] provide a more empirical derivation of effective leadership skills. On the basis of an interview study of over 400 highly effective managers, the following ten skills were identified

1. Verbal communication (including listening)
2. Managing time and stress
3. Managing individual decisions
4. Recognizing, defining, and solving problems
5. Motivating and influencing others
6. Delegating
7. Setting goals and articulating a vision
8. Self-awareness
9. Team building
10. Managing conflict.

Follow-up studies and related research have found skills similar to the ten above. Through statistical techniques, the results of various research studies were combined into the following four categories of effective leadership skills:

1. Participative and human relations
2. Competitiveness and control
3. Innovativeness and entrepreneurship
4. Maintaining order and rationality.[17]

Traits Research and Results

In general, the search for leadership traits has been

largely unsuccessful. It has failed to demonstrate a consistent and definite relationship between leadership ability on one hand and physical traits or personality characteristics or a combination of the two on the other.[18] Byrd,[19] in a critical assessment of research on Trait theory upto 1940, identified a long list of traits made by studies, which had differentiated between leaders and the led. He found that only 5 per cent of the traits listed in them were common to four or more of the studies. Another study by Jennings,[20] concluded: 'fifty years of the study have failed to produce one personality trait or set of qualities that can be used to discriminate between leaders and non-leaders'.

Later studies identified some correlation between leadership and certain personality traits; for example a significant correlation was seen between leadership effectiveness and such traits as intelligence, supervisory ability, initiative, self-assurance and individuality.[21] A definite correlation was observed in some cases between the traits of intelligence, scholarship, dependability, responsibility, social participation and socio-economic status of leaders, as compared with non-leaders.[22] But even these correlations between traits and leadership are not really pervasive. Most of the so-called traits are in essence the pattern of behaviour that one would expect from a leader, particularly in a managerial position.[23]

In general, studies of leader's traits have not been a very fruitful approach to explain leadership. Not all leaders possess all the traits, and many non-leaders may possess most or all of them. Also, the trait approach gives no guidance as to how much of a particular trait a person should have to be a leader. Furthermore, the dozens of studies that have made do not agree as to what traits are leadership traits or what their relationships are to actual instances of leadership. Most of these so-called traits are really patterns of behaviour.

Behavioural Approach to Leadership

When it became evident that effective leaders did not seem to have any distinguished traits or characteristics peculiar to them researchers tried to isolate the behaviours that made leaders effective. In other words, rather than try to figure out what effective leaders were, researchers tried to determine what effective leaders did - how they delegated tasks, how they communicated with and tried to motivate their subordinates, how they carried out their tasks, and so on. Unlike traits, however, behaviours can be learnt; if followed, therefore, that individual trained in appropriate leadership behaviours would be able to lead more effectively[24].

The following are the important studies, which come under the behavioural approach to leadership.

McGregor's Theory 'X' and Theory 'Y'

This theory is related to both leadership and motivation. From the leadership point of view it emphasizes the assumptions of managers regarding the behavioural patterns of subordinates. From the motivation point of view it provides directions to managers to deal with subordinates of different types as perceived by the managers. McGregor identified two major perceptual structures which he labelled 'theory X' and 'theory Y'.[25] The manager who perceives people according to either structure, regardless of whether or not he recognizes or acknowledges such perceptions, will behave in predictable patterns because of his personal assumptions, beliefs and attitudes.

The assumptions about the nature of man which underlie the two theories are as follows;

Theory 'X' assumptions

a) The average human being has an inherent dislike of work and will avoid it if he can.

b) Because of this human characteristic of dislike of work, most people must be coerced, directed, threatened with punishment to get them to put forth adequate effort towards the achievement of organizational objectives.

c) The average human being prefers to be directed, wishes to avoid responsibility, has relatively little ambition and wants security above all.

Theory 'Y' assumptions

a) The average human being does not have inherent dislike of work. Depending upon controllable conditions, work may be a source of satisfaction (and will be voluntarily preferred) or a source of punishment (and will be avoided if possible).

b) External control and threat of punishment are not the only means to bring about efforts towards the organizational objectives. Any person will exercise self-direction and self-control in the service of objectives to which he is committed.

c) Commitment to objectives is a function of the rewards associated with their achievements.

d) The capacity to exercise a relatively high degree of imagination, ingenuity, and creativity in the solution of organizational problems is widely distributed in the population.

e) The average human being learns, under proper conditions, not only to accept but also to seek responsibility.

f) Under the conditions of modern industrial life, the intellectual potentialities of the average human being are only partially utilised.

According to McGregor, the assumptions of a given manager, that may be inferred in his actions, are traced backward from how he must perceive people to cause him to act that way. If he is strongly authoritarian, he insists on giving orders and commands, rather than suggestions and counseling. In this one would predict theory 'x' perceptual structure. The manager who is less aloof; spends time, teaching and training his subordinates emphasizes obtaining results rather than following procedures, and delegates authority, shows signs of embracing theory 'y' assumptions. Thus theory 'x' approximates closely to 'authoritarian', and theory 'y' to 'participative' leadership styles of managing. As an addition to 'x' and 'y', theory 'z' has been introduced.

Theory 'Z'

In contrast to the traditional, more bureaucratic American organization environment, Ouchi[26] recommends a Japanese style Theory 'z' environment. The problem of productivity in the United States will not be solved with monetary policy nor through more investment in research and development. It will only be remedied when we learn how to manage people in such a way that they can work together more effectively.

The characteristics of Theory **'z'** are:

- Long-term, life time-employment;
- Slow process of evaluation and promotion;
- Development of company-specific skills, and moderately specialised career path;
- Implicit, informal control mechanisms supported by explicit, formal measures;
- Participative decision-making by consensus;
- Collective decision-making but individual ultimate responsibility;
- Broad concern for the welfare of subordinates and co-workers as a natural part of a working relationship, and informal relationship among people.

The Lewin, Lippitt and White Study

One of the earliest attempts to delineate the dimensions of leadership behaviour was made by Lewin and others.[27] This research, in addition to triggering off many other studies based on the same model, was also picked by managerial practitioners. As a result of their observations of the behaviour of a small group of children in a laboratory situation, the following three categories of leaders were identified.

a. **The authoritarian leader:** He himself makes all the decisions that relate to the group and is probably the only source of influence in the group's activities. His most effective technique in maintaining this leadership position is by withholding knowledge of goals, not sharing information required for the task, and not providing feedback to members on their progress.

b. **The democratic leader:** He makes decisions jointly with his subordinates, showing his power and influence with the group. The participative process, although time-consuming, effectively encourages each members input and familiarity with the problem. The leader gains additional information from group members as well as a greater commitment to the decision than that would occur under authoritarian conditions.

c. **The laissez-faire leader:** He allows subordinates to make all the decision. His role becomes that of a general supervisor who establishes merely the broad policies and outline of things to be done and then delegates the implementation to his subordinates. As the term, 'laissez-faire' implies, such a leader is a figurehead and makes no contribution to the group goal attainment. No direction is given to the group members.

According to their study of Lewin and others, the democratic style of leadership is more effective than the other styles.

Ohio State Studies

The most comprehensive and replicated of the behavioural theories resulted from research that began at Ohio State University in the late 1940s.[28] These studies sought to identify independent dimensions of leader behaviour. Beginning with over a thousand dimensions, they eventually narrowed the list down to two categories that substantially accounted for most of the leadership behaviour described by subordinates. They called these two dimensions initiating structure and consideration.

The Initiating structure refers to the extent to which a leader is likely to define and structure his or her role and those of subordinates in the search for goal attainment. It includes behaviour that attempts to organize work, work relationships and goals. The leader characterized as high in the initiating structure could be described in terms such as, 'assigns group members to particular tasks'; 'expects workers to maintain definite standards of performance'; 'and emphasizes the meeting of deadlines'.

The Consideration is described as the existent to which a person is likely to have job relationships that are characterized by mutual trust, respect for subordinates' ideas, and regard for their feelings. He shows concern for his follower's comfort, well-being, status and satisfaction. A leader high in consideration could be described as one who helps subordinates with personal problems, being friendly and approachable and treats all subordinates as equals.

Consideration and initiating structures were found to be uncorrelated and independent dimensions. They are separate behavioral categories and give rise to four types of leadership behaviour. Leaders may be

Low on consideration and low on structure;

Low on consideration and high on structure;

High on consideration and high on structure; or

High on consideration and low on structure.

Leadership behaviour could, therefore, be shown on two separate axes instead of along a single continuum. As a result four quadrants were developed which illustrated the different combinations of 'consideration' and 'structure'.

Extensive research based on these definitions, found that leaders high in initiating structure and consideration tended to achieve high subordinate performance and satisfaction more frequently than those who rated low on either consideration, initiating structure or both. The Ohio State studies suggested that the 'high – high' style generally resulted in positive outcomes, but enough exceptions were found to indicate that situational factors needed to be integrated into the theory.

Michigan Studies

Leadership studies undertaken at the university of Michigan's Survey Research Center, at about the same time as those being done at Ohio State, had similar research objectives: to locate behavioural characteristics of leaders that appeared to be related to measure of performance effectiveness. Effective supervisors (measured along dimensions of group morale, productivity and cost reduction) appeared to display four common characteristics:

1. delegation of authority and avoidance of close supervision;
2. interest and concern in their subordinates as individuals;
3. participative problem-solving; and
4. high standards of performance.

The Michigan group came up with two dimensions of leadership behaviour which they labelled 'employee-oriented' and 'production-oriented'.[29] Leaders who were employee-oriented were described as emphasising interpersonal relationships; they took personal interest in the needs of their subordinates and accepted individual differences among members. The production-oriented leaders, in contrast, tended to emphasizing the technical or task aspects of the job keeping their main concern over accomplishing their group's task through the means of group members.

The conclusions arrived at by the Michigan researchers strongly favoured the leaders who were employee-oriented in their behaviour. Employee-oriented leaders were associated with high group productivity and higher job satisfaction. Production-oriented leaders tended to be associated with low group productivity and lower worker satisfaction.

Likert System 4 Management

Rensis Likert,[30] again incorporating the basic style categories of task orientation and employee orientation, devised a four-level model of management effectiveness.

In System 1 managers make all the work-related decisions and order their subordinates to carry them out. Standards and methods of performance are also rigidly set by them. Failure to meet the managers' goals results in threats or punishment. The managers feel little trust or confidence in their subordinates, and the subordinates, in turn, fear the managers and feel that they have little in common with them.

In System 2 managers still issue orders, but their subordinates have some freedom to comment on those orders. The subordinates are also given some flexibility to carry out their tasks but within carefully prescribed limits and procedures. Those subordinates who meet or exceed the manager's goals may be rewarded. In general, the managers have a condescending attitude towards their subordinates, and the subordinates are cautious when dealing with their managers.

In System 3, managers set the goals and issue general orders after discussing them with their subordinates. The subordinates can make their own decisions about how to carry out their task, since only broad and major decisions are made by high-level managers. Rewards, rather than the threats of punishment, are used to motivate the subordinates. The subordinates feel free to discuss most work-related matters with their managers, who, in turn, feel that to a larger extent the subordinates can be trusted to carry out their tasks properly.

System 4 is Likert's ideal system towards which organizations should work. Goals are set and work-related decisions are made by the group. If managers formally reach a decision, they do so after incorporating the suggestions and opinions of the other group members. Thus, the goal they set or the decision they reach may not always be the one they personally favour. To motivate the subordinates, managers not only use economic rewards but also try to give their subordinates the feeling of worth and importance. Performance standards exist to permit self-appraisal by subordinates, rather than to provide the managers with a tool to control them. Interaction between the managers and subordinates is frank, friendly and trusting.

Managerial Grid

The managerial grid identifies a range of management behaviours based on the various ways that task-oriented and employee-oriented styles (each expressed as a continuum on a scale of 1 to 9) can interact with each other.[31] Thus, style 1,1 management is an impoverished management with low concern for people and low concern for tasks or production. This style is some times called laissez-faire management, because the leader abdicates his or her leadership role.

Style 1,9 management is country club management in which there is high concern for employees but low concern for production. Style 9,1 management is task or authoritarian management with high concern for production and efficiency but low concern for employees. Style 5,5 is middle-of-the-road management in which there is an intermediate amount of concern for both production and employee satisfaction.

Style 9,9 management is team or democratic management in which is found a high concern for both production and employee morale and satisfaction. Blake and Mouton argue strongly that the 9, 9 management style is the most effective type of leadership behaviour. This approach will, in almost all situations, result in improved performance, low absenteeism and turnover, and high employee satisfaction.

Leadership Continuum

Another important work on leadership styles is that of Tannenbaum and Schmidt.[32] They suggest a continuum of possible leadership behaviour available to a manager and along which various styles of leadership may be placed. At one extreme of the continuum is the boss-centred leadership (authoritarian) and at the other extreme is the subordinate-centred leadership (democratic).

The continuum presents a range of action related to the degree of authority used by the manager and to the area of freedom available to the subordinates in arriving at decisions. Moving along the continuum, the manager may be characterised according to the degree of control that is maintained over the subordinates. Neither extreme of the continuum is absolute as there is always some limitation on authority and on freedom. This approach can be seen as identifying four main styles of leadership by the manager: tells, sells, consults, and joins.

Tells - the manager identifies the problem, chooses a decision and announces this to his subordinates, expecting them to implement it without an opportunity for participation.

Sells - the manager still chooses a decision but recognises the possibility of some resistance from those faced with the decision and attempts to persuade his subordinates to accept it.

Consults - the manager identifies the problem but does not choose a decision until the problem is presented to the group, and the manager has listened to the advice and solutions suggested by the subordinates.

Joins - the manager defines the problem and the limits within which the decision must be chosen and then passes on to the group, with the manager as a member, the right to make decisions.

Tannenbaum and Schmidt suggested that there are three factors or forces, of particular importance in deciding what types of leadership are practicable and desirable. These are: forces in the manager; forces in the subordinates; forces in the situation

Forces in the manager: The manager's behaviour is influenced by his own personality, background, knowledge and experiences. These internal forces will include: value systems; confidence in subordinates; leadership inclinations; and feelings of security in an uncertain situation.

Forces in the subordinates: The subordinates are influenced by many personality variables and their individual set of expectations about relationship with the manager. Characteristics of the subordinates are: the strength of the needs for independence; the readiness to assume responsibility for decision making; the degree of tolerance for ambiguity; interest in the problem and the feelings as to its importance; understanding and identification with the goals of an organization; necessary knowledge and experience to deal with the problem; and the extent of learning to expect to share in decision making.

Forces in the situation: The manager's behaviour will be influenced by the general situation and environmental pressures. Characteristics in the situation include: type of organization; group effectiveness; nature of the problem; and pressure of time.

Tannenbaum and Schmidt[33] conclude that successful leaders are keenly aware of those factors or forces which are most relevant to their behaviour at a particular time. Successful managers are both perceptive and flexible.

Further, more attention would be given to the interdependency of the forces in the manager. in the subordinates and in the situation.

Contingency Approach to Leadership

The disillusionment with the 'great man', trait and behavioural approaches to understanding leadership has turned the attention to the study of situations and the belief that leaders are the product of given situations. The contingency approaches to leadership attempt

1. to identify which of these factors is most important under a given set of circumstances; and
2. to predict the leadership style that will be most effective under those circumstances.

In this process several theories like Fiedler's Contingency Model, Vroom and Yetton Contingency Model, Path Goal Model, Life Cycle Theory, Tri-Dimensional Model and Learning Model have been advanced though, all of them woven around the theme of 'No Best Way'.

Fiedler's Contingency Model

One of the first leader-situation models was developed by Fiedler[34] in his Contingency theory of leadership effectiveness.

Fiedler suggested that leadership behaviour is dependent upon the favourability of the leadership situation. There are three major variables which determine the favourability of the situation and which affect the leader's role and influence.

Leader-Member Relations - The degree to which the leader is trusted and liked by the group members, and their willingness to follow the leader's guidance.

The task structure - the degree to which the task is clearly defined for the group and the extent to which it can be carried out by detailed instructions.

Position power - the power of the leader by virtue of his position in the organization, and the degree to which the leader can exercise authority to influence. For ex: Rewards and punishments or promotion and demotions.

From these three variables, Fiedler constructed eight combinations of group-task situations through which to relate leadership style. When the situation is very favourable (good leader-member relations, structured task, strong position power) or very unfavourable (poor leader-member relations, unstructured task, weak position power), then a task-oriented leader (low Least Preferred Co-worker-LPC) with a directive controlling style will be more effective. When the situation is moderately favourable and the variables are mixed, then the leader with an interpersonal relationship orientation (high LPC) and a participative approach will be more effective.

Fiedler's Contingency model was based on studies of a wide range of group situations, and concentrated on the relationship between leadership and organizational performance. In order to measure the attitudes of the leader, Fiedler developed a 'least preferred co-worker' (LPC) scale. This measures the rating given by leaders about the person with whom they could work the least well. The questionnaire contained 20 items. Each item was given a single ranking between one to eight points, with eight points indicating the most favourable rating. For example:

Pleasant 8 7 6 5 4 3 2 1 Unpleasant

The LPC score is the sum of the numerical ratings on all the items for the 'least preferred co-worker'. The less critical the rating of the least preferred co-worker and the more favourably evaluated, the higher the leader's LPC score.

Fiedler's work has been subjected to much criticism[35] but it does provide a further dimension to the study of leadership. The best style of leadership will be dependent upon the variable factors in the leadership situation. Fielder argues that leadership effectiveness may be improved by changing the leadership situation. Position power, task structure, leader-member relations can be changed to make the situation more compatible with the characteristics of the leaders.

Vroom and Yetton Contingency Model

Vroom and Yetton[36] base their analysis on two aspects of a leader's decision: its quality and its acceptance.

Decision quality, or rationality, is the effect that the decision has on group performance.

Decision acceptance refers to the motivation and commitment of group members in implementing the decision.

A third consideration is:

The amount of time required to make the decision.

This model suggests five main management decision styles.

Autocratic

A I. The Leader solves the problem or makes the decisions alone using information available at the time.

A II. The Leader obtains information from the subordinates but then decides on solution alone.

Consultative

C I. The problem is shared with the relevant subordinates, individually. The leader then makes the decision which may or may not reflect the influence of subordinates.

C II. The problem is shared with subordinates as a group.

The leader then makes the decision which may or may not reflect the influence of suboridnates.

Group

G I. The problem is shared with subordinates as a group. The leader acts as chairperson, rather than an advocate. Together the leader and subordinates generate and evaluate alternatives and attempt to reach group consensus on a solution.

Vroom and Yetton suggest seven decision rules to help the manager discover the most appropriate leadership style in a given situation. The first three rules protect the quality of decisions and the last four the acceptance of decisions. These rules indicate decision styles that a manager should avoid in a given situation and indicate the use of others. Decision tree charts are introduced to help in the application of the rules and to relate the situation to the appropriate leadership style.

Path-Goal Model

The Path-goal theory of leadership, espoused by House,[37] and House and Dessler[38] together is based on the belief that the individual's motivation is dependent upon the expectations that increased effort to achieve an improved level of performance will be successful, and the expectations that improved performance will be instrumental in obtaining positive rewards and avoiding negative outcomes.

It suggests that the performance of subordinates is affected by the extent to which the manager satisfies their expectations. The Path-goal theory hold that subordinates will see leadership behaviour as a motivating influence to the extent that it satisfies their expectations. Satisfaction of their needs is dependent upon effective performance; and the necessary direction, guidance, training and support, which would otherwise be lacking, are provided.

Remarkably, House identifies four main types of leadership behaviour.

Directive leadership involves letting the subordinates know exactly what is expected of them and giving specific directions to them. The subordinates are expected to follow rules and regulations.

Supportive leadership involves a friendly and approachable manner, displaying concern for the needs and welfare of the subordinates.

Participative leadership involves consulting the subordinates and the evaluation of their opinions and suggestions before the manager makes the decision.

Achievement-oriented leadership involves setting challenging goals for the subordinates, seeking improvement in their performance and showing confidence in their ability to perform well.

This theory suggests that the different types of behaviour can be practised by the same person at different times in varying situations.

Leadership behaviour is determined by two main situational factors: the personal characteristics of subordinates and the nature of the task.

- The personal characteristics of subordinates determine how they will react to the manager's behaviour and the extent to which they see such behaviour as an immediate or potential source of need satisfaction;

- The nature of the task to the extent that it is routine and structured, or non-routine and unstructured.

Effective leadership behaviour is based, therefore, on both the willingness of the manager to help his subordinates and the needs of the subordinates for help. Leader behaviour will be motivational to the extent that it provides the necessary direction, guidance and support, helps clarify path-goal relationships and removes any obstacles, which hinder the attainment of goals. By using one of the four styles of leadership behaviour the manager attempts to influence subordinates' perceptions and motivation, and smooth out the path to their goals.

Life-cycle Theory Leadership

Paul Hersey and Kenneth H. Blanchard[39] have developed a situational theory of leadership. They call it the "Life-Cycle theory". This theory is based on the belief that the most effective leadership style varies with the maturity of followers. Maturity is viewed as consisting of two components, job-related maturity and psychological maturity. Job-related maturity refers to the ability to perform a task. Psychological maturity refers to a person's willingness to perform a job.

Hersey and Blanchard considered task and relationship behaviour as either high or low and then combined them into four specific leadership styles: telling, selling, participating and delegating. They are described as follows:

1. ***Telling*** (high task-low relationship) the leader defines roles and tells people what, how, when and where to do various tasks. It emphasizes directive behaviour.
2. ***Selling*** (high task-high relationship): The leader

provides both directive behaviour and supportive behaviour.

3. ***Participating*** (low task-high relationship): The leader and the follower share in decision-making, with the main role of the leader being facilitating and communicating.
4. ***Delegating*** (low task-low relationship): The leader provides little direction or support.

Four distinct levels of maturity are:

R1: Person is unwilling and unable to perform the job.

R2: Person is unable but willing to perform the job.

R3: Person is able but unwilling to perform the job.

R4: Person is able and willing to perform the job.

The life-cycle theory suggests that as the individual matures, the leadership style will change. When an employee is first brought into an organization, he is considered immature (R1). Therefore, a high task-low relationship style of leadership (telling) is most appropriate to make the employee learn the new job. After he has learned the job, a high task-high relationship style (selling) is most appropriate (R2).

In the third phase, the employee has now matured (R3) to the point of seeking responsibility and taking the initiative to do the job. The leader should provide emotional support, but must not over direct and initiate structure in terms of task completion (participating style).

Finally, as the follower becomes confident, experienced, and self-motivated, the leader can practice a low task - low relationship style (delegating). A fully matured person (R4) expects to be able to operate with minimum influence from the leader. This can be considered a situation in which the follower's maturity and self-direction area substitute for leadership[40]. A person with a high level of skill, experience and self-motivation does not need a leader to structure the job.

The Tri-Dimensional Model

In his 3-D management styles theory, William J. Reddin[41] has stressed the dimensions of effectiveness. In this model, the concept of leadership style is integrated with the situational demands of a specific environment. When the style of a leader is appropriate to a given situation, it is termed as effective. Conversely, when the style is inappropriate to a given situation, it is termed as ineffective. If the effectiveness of a leader's behaviour style depends upon the situation in which it is used, it would follow that any of the basic styles may be effective or ineffective depending on the situation. The difference between effective and ineffective styles often lies not in the actual behaviour of the leader but in the appropriateness of his behaviour to the environment in which it takes place. Thus, essentially, the third dimension in the leader behaviour style syndrome is the environment.

Although effectiveness appears to be in either situation in this model, in reality it should be represented as a continuum. Any given style in a particular situation could fall somewhere in this continuum from 'extremely effective' to 'extremely ineffective'. Effectiveness, therefore, is a matter of degree, and there could be an infinite number rather than only three facets to effective dimension. To illustrate this point, the effectiveness dimension has been divided in quartiles ranging on the effective side from +1 to +4 and on the ineffective side from –1 to –4.

The four effective and four ineffective styles, in essence, show how appropriate a leader's basic style is in a given situation, as seen by his or her followers, superiors, or associates. A model such as the Tri-dimensional leader effectiveness model is distinctive because it does not depict a single ideal leader behaviour style as appropriate in all situations. For example, the high task and high relationship styles are appropriate only in certain situations.

The Learning Model of Leadership

Argyris[42] and his associate Schon[43] recognize a dichotomy in leadership styles. Instead of emphasizing the contingent situations for effectiveness, they have advanced people-oriented style as a learning model and named their conceptual constructs as Model-I versus Model-II or theory-in-use versus theory-espoused.

The two models have been differentiated in terms of governing values, action strategies, consequences on individual and his environment and consequences on learning and group effectiveness. Model-II is normative and ideal and supports that man by himself tends to keep on learning and growing and that his all-round growth is the primary value. But this model lacks supportive empirical evidence.

Charismatic Leadership

Robert House[44] first proposed the theory of charismatic leadership in 1977 based on the research findings of a variety of social science disciplines. His theory suggests that charismatic leaders are likely to have a lot of self-confidence, firm conviction in their beliefs and ideals, and a strong urge to influence people.

Charisma means:

1. A devotion to the specific and exceptional sanctity, heroism, or exemplary character of an individual person, and of the normative patterns revealed or ordained by that person.[45]
2. Endowed with divine grace.[46]

Charismatic leadership means:

1. The process of influencing major changes in the attitudes and assumptions of organization members, and building commitment for the organization's objectives.[47]

2. Leadership that has a magnetic effect on people.[48]

3. In combination with individualized consideration, intellectual stimulation, and inspirational leadership, a component of transformational leadership.[49]

Robert J. House[50] defines charisma in terms of its effects. A charismatic leader, according to House, is any person who brings about certain outcomes to an unusually high degree. The nine charismatic effects are as follows:

i) Group members' trust in the correctness of the leader's beliefs

ii) Similarity of group members' beliefs to those of the leader

iii) Unquestioning acceptance of the leader

iv) Affection for the leader

v) Willing obedience to the leader

vi) Identification with and emulation of the leader

vii) Emotional involvement of the group member or constituent in the mission

viii) Heightened goals of the group member

ix) Feeling on the part of group members that they will be able to accomplish, or contribute to, the accomplishment of the mission.

The characteristics of charismatic leaders which apply to leaders in general are vision, masterful communication skills, ability to inspire trust, ability to make group members feel capable, energy and action orientation, emotional expressiveness and warmth, willingness to take personal risks, use of unconventional strategies, self-promoting personality, propensity to emerge during crisis and minimum internal conflict.[51]

Two behavioural scientists, Rabindra Kanungo and Jay Conger, have tried to 'strip the aura of mysticism from charisma' and 'deal with it strictly as a behaviour process'. According to them, charisma of the leader lies mainly in the eyes of the followers. Attribution of charisma is a result of the interplay between the leader's attributes, and the needs, values and perceptions of his followers. In effect, one man's naked fakir is another's Mahatma.

Conger and Kanungo[52] in their paper, "Toward a Behavioural Theory of Charismatic Leadership in Organizational Settings," have identified several interrelated behavioural components that characterize charismatic vis-à-vis non-charismatic leaders within organizations.

First, charismatic leaders oppose status quo and strive for radical changes, while the non-charismatic leaders try to maintain the status quo. Second, charismatic leaders want their organizations to achieve some ambitious goal which are highly discrepant from the status quo. This component perhaps closest to what others mean by 'vision' of the charismatic leader. The greater the discrepancy between the status quo and the goal advocated by the leader, the greater the propensity of the followers to attribute extraordinary vision to him. Charisma is an attribute of the leader if his advocacy succeeds but madness if it fails.

Charismatic leaders tend to take high personal risks and engage in self-sacrifice. They tend to use unconventional and out-of-the ordinary means to achieve organizational goals. Such behaviour should also be perceived to have high probability of harming the leader's self-interest.

Conger and Kanungo, offer suggestions for identifying potentially charismatic leaders within organizations and developing them through training in various skill areas, such as critical evaluation, communication and empowering other members of the organization. Kunhert and Lewis[53] have labelled leaders as transactional and transformational.

Transactional Vs Transformational Leadership

Yet another perspective on leadership has been called by a number of labels: charismatic leadership, inspirational leadership, symbolic leadership, and transformational leadership.

Burns[54] initially identified two types of political leadership: transactional and transformational. The transactional leadership is more concerned with the management of individuals and centres around the leader's ability to influence his followers to behave in the way he wants in return for something the follower wants. This type of leadership is fairly synonymous with people management in general. The term transformational leadership is defined as "leadership that goes beyond ordinary expectations by transmitting a sense of mission, stimulating learning experiences, and inspiring new ways of thinking". Transformational leadership may manifest itself, as Burns puts it, 'when one or more persons engage with others in such a way that leaders and followers raise one another to higher levels of motivation and morality'.

The more traditional transactional leadership involves an exchange relationship between leaders and followers, but transformational leadership is based more on the leaders' shifting the values, beliefs, and needs of their followers. Bernard Bass[55] concludes that transactional leadership is a prescription for mediocrity and that transformational leadership leads to superior performance in organizations facing demands for renewal and change. He suggests that fostering transformational leadership through policies of recruitment, selection, promotion, training, and development will pay off in the health, well-being, and effective performance of today's organizations.

Tichy and Devanna[56] find that effective transformational leaders share the following characteristics.

a) They identify themselves as change agents.

b) They are courageous.

c) They believe in people.

d) They are value-driven.

e) They are lifelong learners.

f) They have the ability to deal with complexity, ambiguity, and uncertainty.

g) They are visionaries.

Visionary Leadership

Visionary leadership[57] is the ability to create and articulate a realistic, credible, attractive vision of the future for an organization or organizational unit, which grows out of and improves upon the present. This vision, if properly selected and implemented, is so energizing that it "in effect jump-starts the future by calling forth the skills, talents, and resources to make it happen."

Self-Leadership

A unique substitute for leadership is the idea of self-leadership. This process has two thrusts: leading oneself to perform naturally motivating tasks, as well as managing oneself to do work that is required but not naturally rewarding. Self-leadership may involve employees' observing their own behaviour, setting their own goals, cueing themselves to perform, rehearsing effective behaviours, and administering rewards and punishments to themselves.

Social Learning Theory

Social learning theory of leadership can provide a model for the continuous, reciprocal interaction between the leader (including his or her cognitions), the environment (including subordinates/followers and macro-organizational variables), and behaviour itself.[58]

Leadership of Leadership

Charles C. Manz and Henry P. Sims, Jr.[59] have formulated what they refer to as the Super Leadership Theory. A Super Leader is one who leads other leaders by acting as a teacher and a coach, not a director.

A super leader inspires others to motivate themselves and when people are self-directing, they require a minimum of external control.

Super leadership requires the leader to take risks with people: to believe that if given a chance to be self-directing, workers will rise to the occasion.

Leaders and individual contributors alike should be able to practice self-leadership by incorporating the following attitudes and behaviours:

i) Identification and replacement of destructive beliefs and assumptions. Negative thoughts are identified and then replaced with more accurate and constructive ones.

ii) Positive and constructive self-talk. Negative thoughts are converted into positive ones.

iii) Visualization of methods for effective performance. One imagines oneself moving effortlessly through a challenging assignment using methods that have worked in the past.

In summary, the super leader helps create conditions whereby the team members require very little leadership.

Achieving such a goal is important because organizations have reduced the number of managers. Also, organizational structures such as work teams and horizontal structures require a high degree of self-management.

A super leader is one who leads others to lead themselves. Teaching team members to develop productive thought patterns helps develop self-leadership. For example, the leader encourages people to talk to themselves positively and constructively. In this respect since we are studying leadership which is of a global and diverse in nature pertaining to whole mankind, ever relevant and evergrowing in importance we may look into differential perception of leadership.

REFERENCES

1. Fiedler, F.E. "Style or Circumstance: The Leadership Enigma", *Psychology Today*, March, 1969, p.39
2. Vroom, V.H., *The Search for a Theory of Leadership in Contemporary Management: Issues and View Points*, Ed. Joseph W. McGuire, Englewood Cliffs, N.J., Prentice-Hall, 1974, p.396.
3. Ordway Tead, *The Art of Leadership*, McGraw Hill Book Company, Inc. New York, 1953, p.83.
4. Chester I. Barnard, *The Functions of the Executive*, Harvard University Press, Cambridge, 1946, p.260.
5. Henry Fayol, *General and Industrial Management*, Pitman and Sons, London, 1949.
6. George R. Terry, *Principles of Management*, Richard D. Irwin, Inc. Home Wood, Illinois, 1968, pp.461-463.
7. Ralph M. Stogdill, "Personal Factors Associated with Leadership: A Survey of the Literature", *Journal of Psychology*, Jan.1948, pp.35-71.
8. Keith Davis, *Human Behaviour at work*, 4th edition, Mc Graw Hill, New Delhi, 1972, pp.102-104.

9. Chris Argyris, *Executive Leadership*, Harper and Brothers Publishers, New York, 1953, pp.4-5.
10. Harold Koontz and Heinz Weihrich, *Essentials of Management*, 5th Edition, McGraw Hill Series in Management, New York, 1990, p.345.
11. Robert L. Katz, "The Skills of an Effective Administrator," *Harvard Business Review*, September-October 1974, pp.90-102.
12. Yukl, Gary., *Leadership in Organizations*, Prentice Hall, Englewood Cliffs, New Jersey, 1981.
13. Michael J. Marquart and Dean W. Engel, "HRD Competencies for a Shrinking World," *Training and Development*, May 1993, pp.62-64.
14. *Ibid.*, p.63
15. Rabindra M. Kanungo and Sasi Misra, "Managerial Resourcefulness: A Reconceptualization of Management Skills," *Human Relations*, December 1992, pp.1311-1332.
16. David A. Whetten and Kim S. Cameron, *Developing Management Skills*, Harper Collins, New York, 1991, p.8.
17. *Ibid.*, p.11.
18. Gibb, C.A. "Leadership" in *Hand Book of Social Psychology* Edited by Lindzey, G. and Aronson, Vol.4, Addison-Wesley, Mass, 1969, pp.215-229.
19. Byrd, C., *Social Psychology*, Appleton – Century – Crofts, 1940, pp183-188.
20. Jennings, E.E. "The Anatomy of Leadership", *Management of Personnel Quarterly*, Vol.1, Autumn, 1961, p.2.
21. Gheselli, E.E. "Management Talent", *American Psychologist*, Vol.18, Oct, 1963, pp.631-642.
22. Stogdill, R.M. "Personal Factors Associated with Leadership: A Survey of Literature", *Journal of Psychology*, Vol.25, 1948, pp.35-71.

23. Koontz, H. and O' Donnel, C., *Management*, McGraw-Hill, New York, 1976, p.591.

24. James Owen, "The Uses of Leadership Theory", *Michigan Business Review*, Vol.25, No.1, January, 1973, pp.13-19.

25. McGregor, D., *The Human Side of Enterprise*, McGraw-Hill, New York, 1960, pp.33-57.

26. Ouchi, W.G., *Theory Z: How American Business can meet the Japanese Challenge*, Addison-Wesley, 1981. p.4

27. Lewin, K., Lippitt, R. and White, R.K. "Patterns of Aggressive Behaviour in Experimentally Created 'Social Climates'", *Journal of Social Psychology*, Vol.10, 1939, pp.271-299.

28. Steven Kerr, Chester, A. Schniesheim, Charles J. Murphy, and Ralph. M. Stogdill. "Toward a Contingency Theory of Leadership based upon the Consideration and Initiating Structure Literature", *Organizational Behaviour and Human Performance*, August 1974, pp.62-82.

29. Khan, R. and Katz D. "Leadership Practices in Relation to Productivity and Morale" in *Group Dynamics, Research and Theory*, 2nd Ed. D. Cartwright and A. Zander Elonsford, Row, Paterson, New York,. 1960, pp.93-98.

30. Rensis Likert, *New Pattern of Management*, McGraw-Hill, New York, 1961, pp.5-25.

31. Robert R. Blake and Jane S. Mouton., *The Managerial Grid*, (Gulf Publishing, Houston, 1978) Kurt Lewin, Ronald Lippitt and Ralph K. White "Patterns of Aggressive Behaviour in Experimentally Created Social Climates", *Journal of Social Psychology*, Vol.10, No.2, May, 1939, pp.271-299.

32. Tannenbaum, R. and Schmidt, W.H. "How to Choose a Leadership Pattern," *Harvard Business Review*, May-June, 1973. pp.162-175, 178-180.

33. Ibid., *Retrospective Commentary*, pp.166-168.

34. Fiedler, F.E., *A Theory of Leadership Effectiveness*, McGraw-Hill, New York, 1967, pp.43-54.

35. Filley, A.C., House, R.J. and Kerr, S., *Managerial Process and Organizational Behaviour*, 2nd Ed. Scott, Foresman, 1976, p.223.

36. Vroom, V.H. and Yetton, P.W., *Leadership and Decision Making*, University of Pittsburgh Press, 1973, pp.64-69.

37. House, R.J. "A Path-Goal Theory of Leadership Effectiveness", *Administrative Science Quarterly*, Vol.16, Sep.1971, pp.321-338.

38. House R.J. and Dessler G. "The Path-Goal Theory of Leadership", in Hunt J.G. and Larson, L. (Eds) *Contingency Approaches to Leadership*, Souther Illionois, University Press, 1974, pp.43-52.

39. Paul Hersey and Kenneth H. Blanchard, *Management of Organisational Behaviour*, Englewood Cliffs, Prentice Hall, New Jersey, 1979.

40. Steven Kerr and John M. Jermier, "Substitutes for Leadership: Their Meaning and Measurement", *Organisational Behaviour and Human Performance*, December 1978, pp.375-403.

41. Reddin J. William. "The 3-D Management Style Theory," *Training and Development Journal*, April 1967, pp.8-17.

42. Argyris, C. "Theories in Action that Inhibit Individual Leaving", *American Psychologist*, Vol.31, 1976, pp.638-654.

43. Argyris C. Schon D "Theory in Practice", Jossy - Bass, San-Francisco, California, 1974,pp.73-81.

44. Robert J. House, "A 1976 Theory of Charismatic Leadership," in J. G. Hunt and L.L.Larson (Eds.), *Leadership: The Cutting Edge* (Southern Illinois University Press, Carbondale, Illinois, 1977), pp.189-207.

45. Max Weber, cited in S.N. Eisenstadt, *Max Weber: On Charisma and Institution Building*, University of Chicago Press, Chicago, 1968.

46. Bernard M. Bass, "Evolving Perspectives on Charismatic Leadership", in *Charismatic Leaders*, eds. Jay A. Conger,

Rabindra N. Kanungo, et al. (Jossey-Bass, San Francisco, 1988), p.40.

47. Gary A. Yukl, *Leadership in Organisations*, 2nd ed. Prentice Hall, Englewood Cliffs, New Jersey, 1989, p.204.

48. James M. Kouzes and Barry Z. Posner, *The Leadership Challenge: How to Get Extraordinary Things Done in Organizations*, Jossey-Bass, San Francisco, 1987, p.123.

49. Bernard M. Bass, cited in Kenneth E. Clark and Miriam B. Clark (eds.), *Measures of Leadership*, A center for Creative Leadership Book, Leadership Library of America, West Orange, New Jersey, 1990.

50. Robert J. House,"A 1976 Theory of Charismatic Leadership," in J. G. Hunt And L. L. Larson (eds), *Leadership: The Cutting Edge* Southern Illinois University Press, Carbondale, 1977, pp.185-207.

51. Conger, The Charismatic Leader; Jane M. Howell and Bruce Avolio, "The Ethics of Charismatic Leadership: Submission or Liberation?" *The Executive*, May 1992, pp.43-52.

52. Conger, Jam. and Kanungo, R. "Toward A Behavioural Theory of Charismatic Leadership in Organizational Setting," *Academy of Management Review*, Vol.12, No.4, October 1987, pp.637-648.

53. Kunhert, K.W. and Lewis, P. "Transactional and Transformational Leadership: A Constructive and A developmental Analysis," *Academy of Management Review*, Vol.12, No.4, 1987, pp.648-657.

54. J. M. Burns, *Leadership*, Harper and Row, New York, 1978.

55. Bernard M. Bass, "From Transactional to Transformational Leadership: Learning to Share the Vision," *Organizational Dynamics*, Winter 1990, pp.19-31.

56. Noel M. Tichy and Mary Anne Devanna, "The Transformational Leader," *Training and Development Journal*, July 1986, pp.30-32.

57. Nanus. B., *Visionary Leadership*, Free Press, New York, 1992, p.8.

58. Fred Luthans, "Leadership: A Proposal for a Social Learning Theory Base and Observational and Functional Analysis Techniques to Measure Leader Behaviour," in J.G. Hunt And L.L. Larson (Eds.), *Crosscurrents in Leadership*, Southern Illinois University Press, Carbondale and Edwardsville, Illinois, 1979, pp.201-208.

59. Charles C. Manz and Henry P. Sims, Jr., "Super Leadership: Beyond the Myth of Heroic Leadership", *Organizational Dynamics*, Spring 1991, P.18.

3

Review of Literature

Some of the studies made by different authors in both theoretical and empirical spheres are presented hereunder.

Various definitions and concepts of leadership have been reviewed by a number of scholars including Morris and Seeman;[1] Shartle,[2] Carter,[3] Gibb[4] and Bass.[5] From such syntheses the leadership has been defined as an initiation of structure; a locus of group processes; as an art of inducing compliance; as an exercise of influence; as an actor behaviour; as a goal achievement; as an effect of interaction; as a differentiated role, and as a personality and its effects.

The research conducted in the early part of 19th century is replete with identification of certain personality traits essential for leadership. Research studies conducted at the Bureau of Business Research, Ohio State University have attempted to identify initiating structure and consideration.[6]

A series of pioneering leadership studies were conducted on high school children in the late 1930s by Ronald Lippitt and Ralph K. White under the direction of Kurt Lewin at the University of Iowa.[7] They studied the decision-making component of the leader's behaviour and classified leaders into three types as authoritarian, democratic and laissez-faire.

One definite finding was the boys' overwhelming preference for the democratic leader. In individual interviews, nineteen of the twenty boys stated they like the democratic leader better than the authoritarian leader. The boys also chose the laissez-faire leader over the autocratic one in seven out of ten cases.

Leadership studies undertaken at the University of Michigan's Survey Research Centre[8] divide leadership into employee-centered and production-centered. The conclusions arrived at by the Michigan researchers strongly favoured the leaders who were employee-oriented in their behaviour. Employee-oriented leaders were associated with higher group productivity and higher job satisfaction. Production-oriented leader tended to be associated with low group productivity and lower work satisfaction.

In 1945, the Bureau of Business Research at Ohio State University initiated a series of studies on leadership. Stogdill and Coons (1957)[9] were tentatively started with nine dimensions. Factor analysis of the nine subscales revealed two dimensions. They were initiating structure and consideration. The research studies also show that initiating structure and consideration are two separate distinct dimensions and not mutually exclusive. The study found that leaders high in initiating structure and consideration tended to achieve high subordinate performance and satisfaction more frequently than those who rated low either on consideration, initiating structure or both.

Krech and Crutchfield[10] (1948) proposed a number of leadership functions. These are executive, planner, policy-maker, 'expert' external group representative, controller of internal relationships, purveyor of rewards and punishments, arbitrator and mediator, exemplar, symbol of the group, surrogate for individual responsibility, ideologist, father figure and scapegoat.

Hemphill[11] (1949) and his associates at Ohio State Leadership Studies developed a list of approximately 1,800 items describing different aspects of leader behaviour. The items were sorted by the research team into nine different categories or hypothetical subscale, with most items assigned to several subscales. However, 150 items were found on which sorters were agreed to subscale for assigning an item. These items were used to develop the first form of the Leader Behaviour Description Questionnaire (LBDQ).

Robert Tannenbaum and Warren H.Schmidt[12] (1958) see leadership as involving a high variety of styles, ranging from one that is highly boss-centered to one that is highly subordinate–centered. The styles vary with the degree of freedom a leader or manager grants to subordinates. They recognize the following styles:

1. Leader makes decision and announces it.
2. Leader makes decision and persuades subordinates to accept it.
3. Leader presents ideas and invites questions.
4. Leader presents tentative decision subject to change.
5. Leader presents problems, gets ideas and suggestions before making decisions.
6. Leader defines problems and limits of action and asks group to make decisions.
7. Leader permits group to function within limits defined by situations.

The theory recognizes which style of the leader is appropriate depends on the leaders, the followers and the situation and also concludes that the successful leader is one who can assess the forces and behave appropriately at any given time.

Conway[13] (1915) has mentioned three types of Crowd leaders, viz., Crowd-compeller, Crowd-exponent and Crowd-representative.

Bogardus[14] (1918) has suggested four types of leaders:

1. The autocratic type who rises to office in a powerful organization;
2. The democratic type who represents the interests of a group;
3. The executive type who is granted leadership because he can get things done; and
4. The reflective intellectual type who may find it difficult to recruit a large following.

Sanderson and Nafe[15] (1929) have proposed four types of leaders: the static, the executive, the professional and the group leaders. Pigors[16] (1936) has observed that leaders in-group work tend to act either as master or educator.

Levine[17] (1949) has identified four types of leaders. The charismatic leader helps the group rally around a common aim, but tends to become dogmatically rigid. The organizational leader highlights and tends to drive people to effective action. The intellectual leader usually lacks skill in attracting people. The informal leader tends to adopt his style of performance to group needs.

Harding[18] (1949) enumerated twenty types of educational leaders as follows: autocrat, cooperator, elder statesman, eager beaver, pontifical, muddled, loyal staff man, prophet, scientist, mystic, dogmatist, open-minded, philosopher, business expert, benevolent despot, child protector, community-minded, cynic, optimist and democrat.

Maier[19] (1950) investigated the effects of training group leaders in democratic leadership techniques on group problem solving quality and decision acceptance. His subjects role played an assembly line situation, and it was found there from that decision quality and decision acceptance were greater under leaders trained to use democratic techniques than under untrained leaders.

A study by Katz, Maccoby, and Morse[20] (1950) investigated the relationship between the productivity of clerks in an insurance company and various leadership characteristics. Twelve pairs of work groups which performed the same type of work but which differed in their productivity were studied. The supervisors of the high producing groups employed were rated as less 'production centered' and more 'employee centered'; exercised better judgment; were more rational and less arbitrary, and were more democratic and less authoritarian than supervisors of low-producing sections.

Bales[21] (1950) at Harvard and Hare[22] et. al. (1955) had done work on the study of small group. They found that in small groups two different kinds of leaders emerge. One kind was the task-leader characterized by those who talk more and who offer suggestions, and the other kind was called socio-emotional leader represented by those who make it easier for others to talk and offer psychological support. Haiman[23] (1951) suggested that five types of leaders are needed in a democracy. These are: 1. The executive, 2. The judge, 3. The advocate, 4. The expert, and 5. The discussion leader.

Weschler, Kahane and Tannenbaum[24] (1952) studied employees in a naval research laboratory. They found that 63.3 per cent of the members of the division header by the permissive leader were 'well satisfied' with their job, whereas 39.3 per cent of the members of the division headed by the restrictive leader were 'well satisfied' with their job. In addition, the employees' perceptions of morale in their immediate work group, the division, and the laboratory were considerably higher in the permissively run division than in the restrictively run division.

Berkowitz[25] (1953) found that the members of aircrews described the behavior of the aircraft commander in terms of thirteen items. These items were intercorrelated and factor-analyzed. The factors were identified as maintaining standards of performance, behavior in a nurturant manner, acting upon an awareness of situation needs, and maintaining crew coordination and teamwork.

McCurely and Eber[26] (1953) studied groups composed of authoritarian and democratic subjects. Their leaders were coached in either democratic or authoritarian patterns of behavior. Authoritarian groups were somewhat more effective than the democratic groups in speed of problem solving on a group made, although the differences were not significant.

Chowdhry[27] (1953) in her study on difference in worker behaviour associated with low and high tension mills has yielded interesting results regarding the nature of supervisory role. The low tension mills had supervisors of the understanding type who tended to take work through persuasion and felt that workers understand the supervisors message well when addressed in a sweet tongue. The supervisor of high-tension mills used fear to motivate the workers and often observed that he had to give suspension notices in order to warn others to be careful.

Cattell[28] (1954) explored four types of leaders in experimental groups. These are: (1) persistent-momentary problem-solvers, high in interaction rate, (2) salient leaders-picked up by observers as exerting the most powerful influence on the group, (3) socio-metric leaders-nominated by their peers and (4) elected leaders-attaining office by election.

Harris and Fleishman[29] (1955) administered the Leader Behaviour Description Questionnaire to thirty-nine foremen before and after a course on human relations. At the same time, the questionnaire was administered to a control group of foremen who had not taken the course. The control group exhibited greater stability of behaviour over time than the experimental group did, suggesting that training was effective in changing behaviour as perceived by subordinates. However, the trained group exhibited greater change in structure than in consideration.

Shaw[30] (1955) investigated through an experiment, the problem solving performances by four-man groups in different communication nets under authoritarian and democratic leadership. Problems were solved with greater speed and with smaller number of errors under authoritarian leadership. Results also indicated significantly higher morale under democratic leaders than under autocratic leaders. Shaw inferred that morale was heavily influenced by autonomy, which is reduced by authoritarian leadership. Democratic leadership, on the other hand, increased independence and thus morale.

In a study by Baumgartel[31] (1956) three styles of leadership were identified amongst the directors of a laboratory: laissez-faire, directive, and participative. Laissez-faire directors were characterized by little contact and minimal mutual influence between themselves and their subordinates. Directive leaders were in closer contact with their subordinates, exerted considerable influence over their work activities, but were not influenced by their opinions. Finally, participative directors had frequent contact with their subordinates, and were strongly influenced by them. When the work attitudes of research scientists were examined, it was found that those responsible to participative directors expressed more favourable attitudes towards their superiors and their work than did their colleagues whose superiors were laissez-faire or directive. Job satisfaction was found to be higher under participative leaders than under other types of leadership orientations.

Spector and suttell[32] found no difference in group performance under democratic and autocratic leadership. Calvin, Hoffmann and Harden[33] (1957) conducted a series of three group problem solving experiments, comparing democratic and authoritarian leadership styles. They found that no consistent trend emerged in favour of either style. However, their less intelligent subjects performed better under authoritarian leaders, while the more intelligent ones did a shade better under democratic leaders.

Fox[34] (1957) explored the effects of participative, and autocratic leadership styles (he called these as 'positive' and 'negative' styles) on member satisfaction in conference groups. The participative style created more permissive atmosphere, greater member satisfaction with the leader, and easier acceptance of group decisions, as compared to 'negative' or authoritarian leadership style.

Getzels and Guba[35] (1957) proposed three types of leadership; of these two are associated with separate dimensions of group activity. Nomothetic leadership is involved with roles and expectations which define the normative dimensions of activity in social systems. Ideographic leadership is associated with individual needs and dispositions of members which define the personal dimensions of group activity. Synthetic leadership reconciles the conflicting demands arising from the two contrasting systems within a group.

Rambo[36] (1958) found that executives in different departments of an organization differ in consideration and structure. However, no significant differences were found between executives in different echelons of the vertical structure. Stogdill[37] (1959) suggested that it is the function of the leader to maintain group structure and goal direction and to reconcile conflicting demands arising outside the group. Myer[38] (1960) from his interviews with industrialists, government officials, labour leaders and managers in both Indian and foreign-owned firms, concludes that though there are some exceptional companies, many Indian top managements are relatively authoritarian in their relationships with lower managements and with labour.

Lanzetta and Roby[39] (1960) concluded that both time and error scores for problem solving groups were better under participative than authoritarian leadership. The researchers observed, however, that the best performing groups were those in which leadership and power sharing in decision-making was in keeping with the variations in the abilities of members of the group. Thus when the most skilled members of the group used maximum influence in decision-making, the participation was effective.

Vroom[40] (1960), using a sample of 108 supervisors found that participation was significantly correlated with performance for the total sample, but the correlations were significantly higher for supervisors high in autonomy than for supervisor low in autonomy, and for those low in authoritarianism than high in authoritarianism.

A study by Vroom and Mann[41] (1960) investigated the effects of leadership style on employee attitudes. They used two samples of employees. It was found that highly interdependent employees in small work groups having great deal of interaction among themselves, and between themselves and their supervisors had more favourable attitudes toward democratic leaders. Employees had more positive attitudes toward authoritarian leaders. However, in large groups the members of these groups worked independently and there was very little interaction between them and their supervisors.

Douglas McGregor[42] (1960) states that there are four variables involved in leadership: Characteristics of the leader; attitudes, needs and personal characteristics of followers; characteristics of the organization; and the social, economic and political milieu. He also notes that leadership is not a property of the individual, but a complex relationship among these variables. He identifies two major perpetual structures, which are labelled Theory X for the authoritarian approach and Theory Y for the participative approach.

Kidd and Christy[43] (1961) used an air controller simulator and investigated into three types of leader behaviour-autocratic, democratic, and free-reign on several measures of air controller effectiveness. They found that free reign-pattern of leadership allowed the controller to concentrate on maintaining a quick flow through the system but produced high error scores. The autocratic behaviour, on the other hand, reduced the total number of errors and at the same time resulted in inhibiting the rapidity of flow. The participative style was found to result in an intermediary situation.

Chatterjee[44] (1961) obtained high positive correlation between democratic leadership and productivity. Bhatt and Pathak[45] (1962) found high intelligence and dependability as important perceived characteristics of effective supervision. Sequeria[46] (1962), who worked with Ganguli, has outlined the characteristics of the effective supervision. He has come to the conclusion that effective supervisory practice is less ambiguous and less relative. The main criterion seems to be the level of supervisor in the hierarchy.

Amin[47] (1963) reports on the behaviour and traits of jobbers who were liked by the workers. Qualities perceived in successful jobbers were high technical knowledge and ability to co-ordinate supply of materials, good behaviour, politeness and straightforward and persuasive approach. They were not expected to pass on duties to workers under them but were expected to give freedom to workers in their work. A theory of effective management known as "Managerial Grid" was advocated by Blake and Mouton[48] (1964). The two dimensions of effective leadership are concern for people and concern for production. Managerial Grid was popularized depicting five types of styles viz., Impoverished, Task, Team, Country Club and Middle of the Road Managers.

Fiedler[49] (1964) developed a model for leadership effectiveness from the basic proposition that the most effective behaviour for leaders to engage is contingent upon characteristics of the situation. According to him, any managerial situation in an organization can be classified on the basis of the extent of which the situation is favourable to the leader. The factors he found were: leader-member relations, task-structure, and position-power. According to him leader-member relations are good if the leader is respected and accepted by his group. The task is highly structured if it is clearly outlined. The leader's position power is high if he has the power to hire and fire, promote and transfer, increase and decrease salaries.

Anderson[50] (1964) found that those who prefer nursing care activities are described high in consideration. Those supervisors who prefer coordinating activities are not described high in structure. Govindarajan[51] (1964) found significant differences between leaders and non-leaders with regard to vocational preference.

Ganguli[52] (1964) has conducted a study in a state owned engineering company on leadership behaviour. He reported that 46.9 percent of the managers and 31.0 percent of workers of a factory preferred autocratic organizational climate while only 12.30 percent of the managers preferred democratic climate. The existing environment was perceived to be autocratic by 51 percent of the managers and 43.6 percent of the workers.

Apple White[53] (1965) had summarized much of the research on leadership roles and functions, the question of why people attempt to lead, leadership under stress conditions, the relationship of communication to leadership, the problem of leader assessment and the concept of leadership styles.

Stogdill[54] (1965) found in 27 organizations that leader structure is related to follower satisfaction with organization, while consideration is associated with satisfaction with freedom of action.

Meuwese and Fiedler[55] (1965) reported that leaders who are high and low on Fiedler's LPC (Least Preferred Co-worker) measure tend to differ significantly on specific items of the LBDQ (Leader Behaviour Description Questionnaire), but not in the total scores for consideration and structure. Mullen[56] (1965) compared the leadership styles of managers in three divisions of a large automobile insurance company, and its relationship to each division's efficiency and effectiveness. Each manager showed a distinct leadership style: one was democratic, another laissez faire, and the third was authoritarian. It was concluded that all three divisions were operating at an equally high rate of efficiency. Measures of effectiveness did not show any difference between divisions.

Korman[57] (1966) reviewed the research in which consideration and structure scores of industrial supervisors were related to various criteria of supervisory effectiveness and work group performance. It was found that ratings made by peers of supervisory and group performance are not related to the supervisor's consideration and initiation of structure. However, evaluations by superiors and subordinates, as well as various objective criteria tend to be related significantly to the supervisor's leader behaviour as described by subordinates.

Shaw and Blum[58] (1966) assigned eighteen groups of people to either an autocratic or democratic leader where they were given three tasks, different in structure to solve. In terms of time taken to perform the tasks, it was found that autocratic (or directive) leadership was more effective than non-directive (democratic) leadership, when the task was highly structured. Further, unstructured tasks requiring varied information were more effectively solved under the non-directive leadership.

Sinha and Kumar[59] (1966) found student leadership to be related to anxiety and dominance and not to extroversion, neuroticism, adjustment, rigidity and ambiguity tolerance. Rensis Likert[60] (1967) and his associates of University of Michigan have developed four systems of management: Exploitative autocratic (System 1) Benevolent autocratic (System 2), Participative (System 3), and democratic (System 4). On the basis of intensive research, Likert has shown that high producing departments in several organizations are marked by system 4 (democratic).

Yukl[61] (1968) found that task-oriented leaders tend to be described high in structure and low in consideration. Bhusan[62] (1968) in his study concluded that persons in the middle age with higher education and those coming from urban areas have shown significantly greater preference for a democratic style of leadership. Skinner[63] (1969) found that supervisory consideration bears a curvilinear relationship to employee turnover and grievances as consideration increases, grievances decrease to a point and then level off.

Graham[64] (1969) found that high LPC (Least Preferred Co-worker) leaders were described higher in consideration and structure than low LPC leaders. Siegel[65] (1969) found that neither consideration nor structure is related to personality measures, but those managers described high in consideration and structure report higher degrees of need satisfaction. Bayati[66] (1969) investigated into the leader behaviour characteristics of school pupils. He found significant relationship of children's age, parents income and occupations to the patterns of nursery school behaviour.

In a survey by Punekar and Savur[67] (1969) of the relations between white-collar employees and their supervisors in 11 different organizations such as banks, insurance companies, manufacturing firms, government offices, a state–owned public utility company and an educational institution, it was found that only three supervisors out of a sample of 75 believed that subordinates can work without supervision and only six thought that giving responsibility to the white–collar employee is the best way to get the work done. Most supervisors (70%) expressed the belief that subordinates can only work with supervision and have no sense of responsibility.

Sinha and Chowdary[68] (1969) have studied 165 male executives in India to test the effectiveness of leadership style. They have concluded that for less prepared subordinates, nurturant task (NT) leadership style is expected to be used more often and with greater effectiveness, where as for better prepared subordinates, participative leadership style is anticipated to be effectively employed. An authoritarian leader is considered to be ineffective.

Thiagarajan and Deep[69] (1970) found that authoritarian leaders as more influential than the persuasive, and the persuasive more than participative. Evans[70] (1970) tested the path-goal hypothesis in two organizations. It was found that consideration and structure do not interact in path-goal facilitation but, rather, both consideration and structure acted separately to enhance path-goal instrumentality. Fleishman and Simmons[71] (1970) studied the effectiveness of Israeli foremen. Those high in both consideration and structure were most effective. Those low on both scales were least effective.

Sadler[72] (1970) drew a comparison among the various leadership styles preferred by employees in British companies. This involved 1,270 men and 319 women employed by two companies engaged in the marketing of office and computer equipment and in research and development for computer facilities. Employees' preferences were recorded in terms of four leadership styles: 'Tells, Sells, Consults, Joins (i.e. four points in continuum beginning with authoritarian to democratic style). It was found that most employees preferred a 'consults' style (moderate participation) to other styles. However, the highest degree of satisfaction was associated with getting the style of leadership that employees wanted, regardless of the actual style.

Tosi[73] (1970) attempted a study with consumer finance office managers. He found no relationship between perceived participation in decision-making and performance for any group. However, an overall correlation between participative leadership style and job satisfaction was revealed. Katzell[74] et. al. (1970) in a study of groups solving the 'twenty questions' parlor game found that satisfaction with the task was significantly less for those subject under highly directive leaders as compared to leaders who were not so directive. Reddin[75] (1970) conceptualized a three-dimensional grid borrowing some of the ideas from the managerial grid. Three-dimensional axes represent task-orientation, relationship-orientation and effectiveness. By adding an effectiveness dimension to the task–oriented behaviour dimensions, he has integrated the concept of leadership styles with the situational demand of a specific environment.

According to R. J. House theory[76] (1971) (called Path–goal theory) it is the leader's job to assist his followers in attaining their goals and to provide necessary direction and support to ensure that their goals are compatible with the overall objectives of the group or organization. According to path-goal theory when leaders demonstrate high consideration, subordinates are likely to experience greater satisfaction whereas high initiating structure provides role clarity and should lead to higher performance. Four kinds of leadership behaviour are identified under this theory. There are: directive, supportive, participative, and achievement-oriented.

In Japan, Misumi[77] (1972) and his co-workers conducted a number of studies comparing **P** (standing for performance oriented), **M** (for maintaining and strengthening group processes), **PM** (high on both) and **pm** (low on both) types of leadership. When he took into account the level of achievement motivation of his subjects, it was found that regarding the productivity index in the high motivation for achievement group, the **PM** type came out on top, followed by **pm** in that order. In terms of the degree of satisfaction with situation, **PM** came first, followed by **M, P**, and **pm** in the order mentioned.

Wexley[78] et. al. (1973) in an experiment using simulated appraisal interviews discovered a positive relationship between the extent of participation in decision-making and satisfaction with the interview. Brunson and Wickhert[79] (1973) supported the contingency theory and Likert's Participation theory. The most effective division with a short-term orientation and manufacturing goal orientation appeared to be least participative, while the most effective division with the longer-term time orientation and scientific goal orientation appeared to be most participative.

Vroom and Yetton[80] (1973) proposed the leadership participation model. It relates leadership behaviour and participation to decision–making. It provides a sequential set of rules that should be followed in determining the form and amount of participation in decision–making, as determined by different types of situations. Nitish De[81] (1974) has surveyed the value systems of Indian managers and managers of other countries and found that though Indian manager profess a belief in group-based participative decision making, they have little faith in the capacity of workers for taking initiative and responsibility.

In India, Kakar[82] (1974) has found that "though both the assertive and nurturant superior models exist in other areas of social relations in India, it is the nurturant who is held to be the most effective"; and besides, "under highly controlling superiors, the organizational commitment of subordinates with high dependence is positive...."

Elhance and Agarwal[83] (1975) have analyzed the leadership behaviour taking different variables affecting leadership styles along with delegation of authority of 123 executives at various levels of management from two private and two public sector undertakings. They concluded that 67 percent executives in private sector and 57 percent of them in public sector units have employed democratic leadership styles.

R. Rangaswamy and Helmick[84] (1976) in their study of leadership behaviour of 56 top level managers have found that Indian managers are more employee-oriented as compared to their American counterpart. This is due to Indian culture and religious pattern which influence helpfulness and peaceful co-operation.

Sinha[85] (1976) hypothesized that before an organization achieves moderate degree of productivity, it requires nurturant-task orientation style of leadership which can move employees towards harder efforts and work commitment. Once at least when a moderate level of productivity is achieved and the normative structure of the organization are interjected in employees, the organization is ready for the participative style of management.

Kumar and Singh[86] (1976) reported, "Authoritarian leadership is no less preferred than the participative style". R. Lokhande and S.N.singh's[87] (1977) study covers five leadership patterns: 1. Traditional leadership 2. Political leadership 3. Opinion-making leadership, 4. Decision–making leadership and 5. Caste leadership. The study brings out the fact that there have been very poor growth and development of leadership in the villages under study. Socio-economic status, however, has been found to influence considerably the leadership structure with respect to extension programmes. Traditional leadership positively associated with caste and socio-economic status still seems to dominate the form of leadership in village life.

Verma[88] (1977) constructed a Likert type scale to measure authoritarian (F), nurturant-task (NT) and participative (P) styles of student leaders while the coefficient of correlation between F and NT, NT and P and F and P was 0.31, 0.39, and 0.11 respectively. The study by Joseph and Kasavan[89] (1977) of 45 supervisors from public sector and 38 from private sector shows that in a private sector the emphasis is on production which is meaningful since total wages are tied up with the amount produced, whereas in public sector, superior orientation is prevalent which can be explained by the fact that superiors are given complete authority in recommending their subordinates for promotion along with increase in pay.

Singh and Das[90] (1977) in the study of 280 managers from two public sector and four private sector units found that "bureaucratic" style is the most predominant followed by the 'benevolent autocrat' 'developer' and 'democratic' styles of leadership. Further, Singh and Das highlighted that leadership style is associated with the type of organization, executives age group, their level in the organization and their exposure to management programmes. More importantly, according to Singh and Das, in public sector, leadership styles are in order to 'compromiser', 'developer', and 'autocratic' style. In private sector 'benevolent autocracy' is followed by the 'bureaucratic', 'democratic' and 'developer' styles. Hierarchy-wise, top-level managers are more 'benevolent autocrats' followed by 'democratic' and 'developer' in behaviour. While middle and lower level managers are more 'bureaucratic' followed by the 'benevolent autocrat' category. Age-wise, aged managers are more 'benevolent autocratic', followed by 'developer', 'bureaucratic' and 'democratic' leaders; younger executives are more democratic followed by 'benevolent autocratic' and 'bureaucratic'. The executives who are exposed to some formal management education are more democratic as compared to those who do not have such exposure.

Schuler[91] (1977) in a study of manufacturing employees found no overall correlation between participative decision-making and performance. S. Selvadurai[92] (1977) conducted a study on 40 co-operative leaders in Kerala, India, finds that leaders are not made, but evolve depending upon various situations. This study also reveals that there is a positive correlation between the importance a person enjoys in the society and his chances of emerging as a leader in a co-operative.

The findings of Sinha and Sinha[93] (1977) study indicated that the NT leaders were close to the authoritarian leaders in being strict, in pushing their ideas through and in controlling other ideas and activities. The NT leaders were close to the participative ones in encouraging the members, giving due share to their ideas, and yet maintaining control over them. Further, Sinha and Sinha used a semantic differential scale having 20 bipolar adjectives to know the patterns of perceptual set of college students for authoritarian (F), nurturant-task (NT) and participative (P) style of a leader. Besides, they also aim to know the extent to which the subordinates attach stronger evaluative meanings to the three styles. They have stated their findings in the following manner:

> "The authoritarian leader was perceived to be autocratic, influential and brave, yet he was reported to be relatively insecure, impractical, unsuccessful, unskillful, dissatisfying disrespected and unpleasant. The NT leader was perceived to be active, strong, dominant, firm, independent, alert, encouraging, scientific, extrovert and on the whole good. The participative leader was rated to be democratic, respected

and satisfying, secured, skilful, practical and successful. He was also perceived to be relatively weak, a coward, slack and uninfluential".

The study of 120 managers by Jaggi[94] (1978) concludes that prevailing leadership styles appear to be between 'benevolent autocracy' and 'consultative' type. The study further indicates that the leadership style is associated with various factors such as age of the executives, their positions and functions and the size of the organizations. Thus, younger managers and managers in bigger sized companies are less authoritarian whereas the managers in production and technical areas are more authoritarian.

Singh[95] (1979) has studied 100 managers of Public Sector Enterprises and concluded that 3 per cent of managers adapted democratic style, 7 per cent autocratic style, 23 percent compromiser style, 31 percent bureaucratic style and 21 percent developer style. He has found that there is procedural rigidity in Public Sector Enterprises. Kalra[96] (1980) has studied the pattern of styles of 70 managers and has found that most of the managers have their leadership behaviour guided by the situations in their organizations. Sinha[97] (1980) in his study lists out three types of leadership styles as 1.Participative. 2. Authoritarian and 3. Nurturant-task leadership.

Habibullah and Sinha[98] (1980) studied five hundred and twenty-three executives of the Bharath Heavy Electrical Limited to find out various factors of leader behaviour. The responses of the executives to the leadership styles scales were factor analyzed by the principal component method and varimax rotation was used. Resultantly, they found the following ten usable factors: subordinate based participation; leader centered nurturance; authoritarianism; guidance and encouragement; direction; task-orientation; friendly-orientation; power; role performance, distance and discipline.

Jain[99] (1982) studied leadership styles of six district collectors and the rating of 70 subordinates. The collectors self-perception and the subordinates' rating showed more than 60 per cent of acceptance. Only in 2 of the six cases, discrepance was reported. Swarna Pratap and Srivastava[100] (1985) have studied leadership styles and the effectiveness of executives in private, public and governmental sectors. The study is based on Hersey and Blanchard model. They have taken a sample of 80 executives out of which 30 were from private sector. 25 each from public sector and government sectors the study states that much difference in leadership effectiveness and styles in different organizations are not seen. Results on high task–low relationship (style 1) and low task–high relationship (style 3) show that the Indian executives do think on the lines of " concern for the people" but many of them still like to be benevolent autocrats rather than participative managers. High task relationship (style 2) is found to be predominant among executives of organizations. The positive correlations of low task–high relationship (style 3) states that efforts in the direction of participation may be successful.

Muttayya and Vijaya Kumar[101] (1985) by taking a sample of 68 scientific personnel belonging to different research institutions have identified five styles. They are 1. Direction style, 2. Negotiating style, 3. Consultative style, 4. Participative style and 5. Delegation style. The study indicates that the predominant style is 'direction' followed by 'delegation' and participation.

Ramakanth[102] (1985) has made an attempt to know the attitudes of managers in different manufacturing organizations with regard to the classical or modern point of view. He has used a questionnaire covering four distinct areas: 1. Capacity for leadership initiative 2. sharing information and objectives, 3. Participation and 4. Internal control. On the basis of responses, he concludes that in the areas of capacity for leadership initiative, sharing information and objectives and participation, the managers are in favour of modern approach and in the area of internal control, they are in favour of classical approach.

R.P.Singh and Janak Pandey[103] (1986) conducted a study to show pattern of relationship between three leadership styles (participative, authoritarian and authoritative) with different strategies of control, need-satisfaction and commitment with the organization. The study was conducted on a sample of 250 respondents comprising 150 workers, 50 supervisors and 50 line–managers of electronic equipment manufacturing large public undertaking in India. The study suggests that participative style leads to greater need–satisfaction and organizational commitment, and authoritative style is closer to participative leadership but it does not lead to commitment. The study also brings out that participative and authoritative are positive styles of leadership. Authoritative may substitute participative till conditions in an organization do not permit but participative style of leadership would not work till there is change in the sociocultural milieu of the Indian Organizations.

Ansari[104] (1986) observes that NT (Nurturant-Task) is a forerunner of a 'participative' style in the reciprocal influence process between leaders and subordinates. Neelam Varma[105] (1986) has made an attempt to examine the relative validity of the implicit leadership by testing two groups experienced (executives) and inexperienced (students) in an oil refinery. The study suggests that a leader's behaviour may be conceived of as a joint effect of all the five dimensions of leadership, i.e., Authoritarian style, Bureaucratic style, Nurturant, Participative and Task-orientation.

Hingar[106] (1986), in her study found that leadership styles do not exert much influence on job satisfaction. She also found that there is no difference in the leadership styles across managerial hierarchy and there is no difference in the judgement made by leader himself and by his subordinates. Prabhakar Singh[107] (1987) has made an attempt to study the leader behaviours that exist in ineffective and effective organizations producing similar commodity and located in the same area geographically and socially. The study indicates that the leadership that exists in ineffective organization, at all the three levels (lower, middle and upper level executives) does not have any definite and significant trend. The study indicates that significantly high percentage of the executives practiced non-complimentary orientations in leading their subordinates. The executives of effective organization showed a different orientation. The lower management cadre executives showed Nurturant-Task leadership, middle management cadre executives showed Participative-Task-orientation and upper cadre executive showed Participative-Task leadership styles. The study concludes that the Nurturant–task leadership is best leader behaviour for supervising the workmen and Participative–Task leadership is for supervising the executives. The study also indicates that organization, its objectives, culture and values decide to a large extent the type of leader behaviour that its executives shall learn and practice.

Kapila[108] (1987) conducted a study in a large Public Sector steel company on 629 managers and found that autocratic style is the most prominent among work division managers. The other leadership styles such as deserter, executive and developer are the dominant styles. He has concluded that the leadership styles and executives varied with managerial hierarchy. His study showed that smaller age group executives have ineffective styles like deserter and autocratic, middle aged managers have autocratic and executive and older managers have executive and compromiser styles.

Rama Murthy's[109] (1987) study concluded that State Enterprises are dominated by executives with bureaucratic style. Lynn R. Anderson's[110] (1990) study describes two types of leadership training that are most appropriate for high and low self–monitoring individuals: Techniques requiring leaders to change their own behaviours (Track I training) and techniques requiring leaders to change conditions within their organizational environment (Track II training). The study indicates that the personality typology of high versus low self–monitoring is presented as a possible moderator of leadership training. The behaviour of high self–monitoring individuals is guided by situational factors. These leaders should benefit most from leadership training requiring leaders' behaviour to change as a function of group contingencies (Track I training). The behaviour of low self-monitoring individuals is displayed in accordance with internal, dispositional traits and values. These leaders should profit most from thinking that instructs leaders to alter organizational structures to produce an effective match between the leader's intrinsic behavioural style and group contingencies (Track II training).

R.Venkatapathy[111] (1990) views leadership style from three perceptions: benevolent, critical and developmental. His study is based on the assumption that a leader adopting a particular style would create a climate similar to that style. The study is based on the data collected from 6 public sector organizations and 5 private sector organizations represented by 37 executives in each sector. It is concluded that there is no difference among public - private executives on their perception of top management style as Benevolent; significant differences exist on critical and developmental styles but developmental is the primary style followed by Benevolent and critical styles and the perception of public and private executives on climate created by the top management due to their style remains heterogeneous.

In a study by Omer Bin Sayeed[112] (1990) attempted to examine conflict handling strategies, leadership behaviour and leadership styles (relationship and task-motivated styles) in a common framework. The study was conducted on 79 middle level managers who were undergoing various training programmes conducted at National Institute for Training in Industrial Engineering, Bombay, India. It was found that conflict management strategies represented two main conflict management styles, viz., Reciprocal Problem Solving Style and Authoritative System Supported Style, which tended to relate selectively with five leadership dimensions. Reciprocal conflict management style significantly related with Participative, Nurturant, and Task-oriented leadership behavior, while Authoritative Conflict Management Style had significant relationships with authoritarian and bureaucratic leadership behavior. The low esteem for coworker (task-motivated leadership style) had a strong relationship with the application of force as a conflict management strategy, besides revealing some moderating influences of esteem for coworker between leadership behavior and conflict management strategies.

Rama J. Joshi[113] (1991) explores the concept of managerial effectiveness as perceived by the Chief Executives. Based on interviews with the Chief Executives of units (covered by the study), certain dimensions of managerial effectiveness were identified. They are:

Leadership, inspiring, dynamic, motivating, gets respect of others, result oriented, desire to achieve, direct resources towards maximizing results,

Ability with people, good human relations skill, concern for people, identification with the company and its goals.

Understanding and discharging their own role in the organization, effective handling of problems/situations,

Innovative/doing something on their own initiative/ creative

Rajinder Kaur[114] (1993) has designed a study to investigate the psychological characteristics of democratic and autocratic managers as well as to find out the relationship between managerial styles and managerial success. 325 managers from Bharat Electronics Limited, Banaglore comprised the sample. The study indicates that managerial success is not associated with managerial styles. A tendency towards the autocratic style prevails among the Indian managers. The psychological correlates reveal a qualitative difference in the characteristics of the democratic and the autocratic managers.

N. Panchanatham and others[115] (1993) attempted to explore the leadership and problem solving styles of executives of public sector organizations. The results indicate that the executives dominantly used democratic, authoritative and coaching styles of leadership, there were no significant relationships between leadership styles and problem solving styles and in the field of specialization of executives did not have any influence on their problem solving styles. The study suggested that the organization should design separate training programmes on problem solving and leadership styles and the executives of different branches should be considered equally for developmental programmes.

Manisha Agarwal and G.C.Agarwals'[116] (1995) study examined the relationship between junior and middle manager's power styles and their influence over different dimensions of decision-making activities through participativeness in three industrial organizations. Data analysis reveals the importance of the integrated power style in predicting managerial participativeness in goal–setting and conflict-handling. Findings have significant implications for reducing middle level managers' feelings of powerlessness by increasing the degree of their participation in activities affecting personal or organizational level outcomes with the utilization of an integrative approach to power exercise at the work place. The study also indicates the importance of monetary incentives for middle and junior managers for securing their effective participation in the decision–making activities.

S.Subramanian and K.Sajjan Raos'[117] (1997) study is an attempt to investigate the attitudes of union leaders towards certain management decisions. Data have been gathered from 68 union leaders belonging to two prominent unions. Their perceived importance of the 12 crucial management activities and also their perceived contribution of the unions (as opposed to management) in implementing these aspects have been studied. Results reveal a positive orientation of union leaders towards these aspects and suggest that unions have metamorphosed from their traditional role of just getting their colleagues their due, to a more progressive outlook. The authors envisage a more dynamic functioning for union leaders in the changing realities by which they can contribute not only to the welfare of their colleagues, but also towards development of their organization.

V. Ravichandran and D.Nagabrahmam's[118] (1997) study attempted to explore the effectiveness of leadership in a transitory environment. A list of 15 traits/skills such as vision, expertise, motivation, calculated-risk, innovativeness, exemplary, assertion, integrity, charisma, interpersonal skills, initiativeness, ambition, altruism, commitment and empathy were identified through interaction process based on which a questionnaire was constructed and rated on five-point Likert scale. Data were collected from 299 managers representing 8 nationalized banks and their branches. The study states that effective leadership was perceived to be related to the person and his character such as one's expertise with interpersonal capabilities and empathy. The study also suggests that effective leaders are those with vision and having noble and altruistic goals. It is also noted that the ideal of leadership in everybody's mind has influencing effect on leadership in organizations if it is properly communicated and shared among top echelons.

Syed Vazith Hussain[119] (2002) made an attempt to analyse different leadership styles in small scale industries at micro level. The decision making styles are identified by him are: Style I Benevolent autocrat; Style II Strict autocrat; Style III Prior consultation; Style IV Democratic style and Style V Delegation. He collected data from 98 owner-managers of small scale industries. He concluded that owner-managers in small scale industries are adopting different styles depending upon the situation even though they are free from adopting any style. The results of the study strongly confirms the view that leadership is situational and effective leader should be flexible enough to adopt to the differences among the subordinates and situations.

Research Methodology

The purpose of the study is to examine the leadership styles as perceived by the leader himself, subordinates' perception of their superior's leadership styles and leadership concepts and constructs in Bharath Earth Movers Limited (BEML), K.G.F. division, Kolar district, Karnataka.

The specific objectives of the study are to examine the view point of the employees of BEML on Leadership Concepts and Constructs in their organization, the relationship of Leadership Styles with certain Socio-Economic Organizational Position (SEOP) variables and the relationship between Leadership Styles of the employees in BEML;

Hypotheses

The following null hypotheses were formulated and tested for the study:

H1 There is no significant relationship between Leadership Styles and the SEOP variables of employees in BEML.

H1 There is no significant relationship between Leadership Styles of employees in BEML.

H1 There is no significant relationship between SEOP variables of employees in BEML.

The study is based on primary data collected from the employees of BEML. The employees of BEML are categorized as workers, supervisors and officers. The data was collected and categorized as Higher level managers, Middle level managers and Lower level managers. By adopting simple random sampling, from each level of officers 50 per cent are drawn as the sample and the total sample for the study consists of 399 out of 784 officers.

In the present study, four schedules were used to collect the data. Schedule-I was designed to elicit the information relating to the SEOP variables viz., name, age, designation, experience, educational qualifications and economic background. Schedule-II was designed to know the opinion of the respondents regarding on leadership concepts and constructs. Schedule-III, Leader Satisfaction Score (Sinha 1980) which was administered to officers with a view to judging their own leadership styles, and Schedule-IV was designed to measure the leader's style as perceived by his subordinates (Leader Behaviour Score) among officers. Both consists of 50 items each to measure five leadership styles viz., Authoritarian, Participative, Bureaucratic, Task oriented and Nurturant and each of these categories consists of 10 items. Responses were solicited on a 5-point scale, ranging from Quite True (5), True (4), Doubtful (3), False (2), to Quite False(1).

The data collected through the schedules were processed and the results were tested with the hypotheses by employing appropriate statistical tools like percentages and correlation.

REFERENCES

1. Morris, W.T. and Seeman, M. "The Problem of Leadership: An Interdisciplinary Approach," *American Journal of Sociology*, 56 (1950), pp.149-155.
2. Shartle, C.L. "Studies in Naval Leadership," in H. Guetzkow Groups, *Leadership and Men*, Carnegie Press, Pittsburgh, 1951.
3. Carter, L.F. "Leadership and Small Group Behaviour," in M. Sheriff and M.O. Wilson, eds., *Group Relations at the Crossroads*, Harper, 1953.
4. Gibb, C.A. "Leadership," in G. Lindzey and others., *Handbook of Social Psychology*, Addison-Wesley, Mass, 1954.
5. Bass, B. M., *Leadership, Psychology and Organizational Behaviour*, Harper, New York, 1960.
6. Stogdill, R.M. and Coons, A.E. (Ed) "Leader Behaviour: Its Description and Measurement," *Research Monograph No.88*, Bureau of Business Research, Ohio State University, Columbus, 1957.
7. Lewin, Lippitt, R., and White, R.K. "Patterns of Aggressive Behaviour in Experimentally Created 'Social Climates'," *Journal of Psychology*, 1939, pp.271-299.
8. Daniel Katz et al. *Productivity, Supervision and Morale in Office Situation*, Survey Research Centre, University of Michigan, Ann Arbor, 1950.
9. Stogdill, R.M. and Coons. A.E. (Eds.) "Leader Behaviour: Its Perception and Measurement," Bureau of Business Research, Ohio State University, Columbus, 1957.
10. Krech, E. and Crutchfield, R.S., *Theory and Problems of Social Psychology*, McGraw Hill, New York, 1948.
11. Hemphill, J.K. "The Leader and his Group," *Journal of Educational Research*, 28 (1949).
12. Robert Tannenbaum and Warren H. Schmidt "How to choose a Leadership Pattern," *Harvard Business Review*

(March – April 1958), pp.95-101, and Heinz Weihrich, "How to Change a Leadership pattern," *Management Review* (April 1979) pp.26-28, 37-40.

13. Conway, M., *The Crown in Peace and War*, Longmans Green, New York, 1915.

14. Bogardus, E.S., *Essentials of Social Psychology*, University of Southern California Press, Los Angels, 1918.

15. Sanderson, D. and Nafe, R.W. "Studies in Rural Leadership," *Publ. Amer. Social. Soc.*, 23 (1929), pp.163-175.

16. Pigors, P. "Types of Leaders in Group Work," *Sociology and Social Research*, 21 (1936), pp.3-17.

17. Levine, S. "An Approach to Constructive Leadership," *Journal of Sociological Issues,* 5 (1949), 46-53.

18. Harding, L. W. "Twenty-One Varieties of Educational Leadership," *Educational Leadership,* 6 (1949), pp. 299-302.

19. Maier, N.F.R. "The Quality of Group Decisions as Influenced by the Discussion Leader," *Human Relations*, 6, (1950), pp.161-173.

20. Katz. D.N., Maccoby and Morse, N. *Productivity, Supervision, and Morale in an Office Situation*, Survey Research Center, Institute for Social Research, University of Michigan, Ann Arber, Michigan, 1950.

21. Bales, R.F. "Interaction Process Analysis: A Method for the study of Small Groups," Cambridge, 1950.

22. Hare, A.P. Borgatta, E.E., and Bales, R.F. "Small Groups Studies in Social Group Interaction," New York, 1955.

23. Haiman, F.S., *Group Leadership and Democratic Action*, Houghton Mifflin, Boston, 1951.

24. Weschler, J.R., Kahane, M., and Tannenbaum, R. "Job Satisfaction, Productivity, and Morale: A Case Study," *Occupational Psychology*,26, (1952), pp.1-14.

25. Berkowitz, L. "An Exploratory Study of the Roles of Aircraft Commanders," USAF *Human Resource Research Center, Research Bulletin*, 56-65 (1953), pp.1-27.

26. McCurely, H.G., and Eber, H.W. "Democratic Versus Authoritarian: A Further Investigation of Group Problem Solving," *Journal of Personality*, 22, (1953), pp.258-269.

27. Chowdhry, K. "An analysis of the Attitudes of Textile Workers and the Effects of those Attitudes on Work Efficiency," *Human Relation Division Research Note.*, ATIRA, 3 (1953).

28. Cattell, R.B. and Stice, G.F. "Four formulae for Selecting Leaders on the basis of Personality," *Human Relations*, 7 (1954).

29. Harris, E.F. and Fleishman, E.A. "Human Relations Training and the Stability of Leadership Patterns," *Journal of Applied Psychology*, 39 (1955).

30. Shaw, M.E. "A Comparison of two types of Leadership in Various Communication Nets," *Journal of Abnormal and Social Psychology*, 50, (1955), pp.127-134.

31. Baumgartel, H. "Leadership, Motivations and Attitudes in Research Laboratories," *Journal of Social Issues*, 12, (1956), pp.24-31.

32. Spector, P. and Suttell Barbara, J. *Research on the specific leader behaviour patterns most effective in influencing group performance*, American Institute for Research, Washington, D.C., 1956.

33. Calvin, A.D., Hoffmann, F.K. and Harden, E.L. "The Effect of Intelligence and Social Atmosphere on Group Problem Solving Behavior," *Journal of Social Psychology*, 45, (1957), pp.61-74.

34. Fox, W.M. "Group Reaction to two types of Conference Leadership," *Human Relations*, 10, 1957, pp.279-289.

35. Getzels, J.S. and Guba E.G. "Social Behaviour and the Administrative Process," *School Review*, 55 (1957).

36. Rambo, W.W. "The Construction and analysis of a Leadership Behavior Rating Form," *Journal of Applied Psychology*, 42 (1958), pp.409-415.

37. Stogdill, R.M., *Individual Behaviour and Group Achievement*, Oxford University Press, New York, 1959.

38. C.A. Myer, *Industrial Relations in India*, Asia Publishing House, Bombay, 1960, p.166.

39. Lanzetta, J.T. and Roby, T.B. "The Relationship Between Certain Group Process Variables and Group Problem Solving Efficiency," *Journal of Social Psychology*, 52, (1960), pp.135-148.

40. Vroom, V., *Some Personality Determinants of the Effects of Participation*, Prentice Hall, Englewood Cliffs, N.J., 1960.

41. Vroom, V. and Mann, F. "Leader Authoritarianism and Employee Attitudes," *Personnel Psychology*, 13 (1960), pp.125-140.

42. Douglas McGregor, *The Human Side of Enterprise*, McGraw Hill Book Company, New York, 1960.

43. Kidd, J.S., and Christy, R.T. "Supervisory Procedures and Work Team Productivity," *Journal of Applied Psychology*, 45, (1961), pp.388-392.

44. Chatterjee, A. "Satisfaction and Productivity: A Study of Morale and Team Work in Industry with Respect of Productivity," I.I.S. Ph. D. Thesis, Bangalore, 1961.

45. Bhatt L. J. and Pathak, N.S. "A Study of Functions of Supervisory Staff and Characteristics Essential for Success as viewed by a Group of Supervisors," *Manas*, 9 (1962), pp.25-31.

46. Sequeria, C.E. "Functions of a Supervisor," *Indian Journal of Applied Psychology*, 1, (1962), pp.46-54.

47. Amin, D.L. "Perception of the First Line Supervisor about His Job," *Industrial Relations*, IIBM, Calcutta, 1963.

48. Blake, R.R. and Mouton, S.J., *The Managerial Grid*, Gulf Publishing Company, Houston, Taxaus, 1964.

49. Fiedler, F.E. "A Contingency Model of Leadership Effectiveness," Berkowitz (Ed.), Advances in Experimental Social Psychology, Academic Press, New York, 1964.

50. Anderson, L.R. "Some Effects of Leadership Training on Intercultural Discussion Groups," University of Illinois, Group Effectiveness Research Laboratory, Technical Report, Urbana, (1964).

51. Govindarajan, T.N. "A Study of Juvenile Delinquents Position in the Family," *Indian Journal of Applied Psychology*, 3 (1964), pp.56-63.

52. Ganguli, H.C., *Structure and Process of Organisation*, Asia Publishing House, Bombay, 1964.

53. Apple White, Phillip B., *Organisational Behaviour*, Engle Wood Cliffs, Prentice-Hall, New Jersey, 1965 (Chapter 6).

54. Stogdill, R.M. "Managers, Employees, Organisations," Bureau of Business Research, Ohio State University, Columbus, 1965.

55. Meuwese, W.A.T. and Fiedler, F.E. "Leadership and Group Creativity under varying conditions of Stress," University of Illinois, Group Effectiveness Research Laboratory, Technical Report, Urbana 1965.

56. Mullen, J.H. "Differential Leadership Modes and Productivity in a Large Organization," *Academy of Management Journal*, 3 (1965), pp.107-126.

57. Korman, A.K. "Consideration, Initiating Structure and Organizational Criteria: A review," *Personnel Psychology*, 19 (1966).

58. Shaw, M.E., and Blum, J.M. "Effects of Leadership Style upon Group Performance as a Function of Task Structure," *Journal of Personality and Social Psychology*, 1966, pp.238-242.

59. Sinha, D. and Kumar, P. "A Study of Certain Personality Variables in Student Leadership," *Psychological Studies*, 11 (1966), pp.1-8.

60. Rensis Likert, *The Human Organization*, McGraw Hill, New York, 1967, P.47.

61. Yukl, G.A. "Leader Personality and Situational Variables as Co-Determinants of Leader Behavior," *Dissertation Abstract*, 29 (1968), p.406.

62. Bhusan, L.I. "Leadership Performance as related to Age, Education, Residence and Sex," *Indian Journal of Social Work*, July, Volume 1, (1968), pp.193-196.

63. Skinner, Elizabeth, W. "Relationships between Leadership Behaviour Patterns and Organizational Situational Variables," *Personnel Psychology*, 22 (1969), pp.489-494.

64. Graham, W.K. "Leader Behavior, Esteem for Least-Preferred Co-Worker, and Group Performance," *American Psychological Association*, 1968, pp.33-40.

65. Siegel, J. P. "A Study of the Relationship among Organizational Factors, Personality Traits, Job and Leadership Attitudes," *Dissertation Abstracts*, 29 (1969), pp.2662-2663.

66. Bayati, J.L. "An Investigation into the Leader Behavior Characteristics of Higher Secondary School Pupils," *Journal of College Education*, Karnataka University, Dharwar, 6 (1969), pp.17-20.

67. S.D. Punekar and M.G.Savur, *Management - White Collar Relations*, Popular Prakashan, Bombay, 1969.

68. Sinha, J.B.P. and Chowdary, G.P. "Perception of Subordinates as a Moderator of Leadership Effectiveness," A.N.S. Institute of Social Studies, Patna, 1979(mimeographed).

69. Thiagarajan, K.M. and Deep, S.D. "A Study of Supervisor Subordinate Influence on Satisfaction in four Cultures," *Journal of Social Psychology*, 82 (1970), 173-180.

70. Evans, M.G. "The Effect of Supervisory Behaviour on the Path-Goal Relationship," *Organizational Behaviour and Human Performance*, 5 (1970), pp.277-297.

71. Fleishman, E.A. and Simmons, J. "Relationship between Leadership Patterns and Effectiveness ratings among Israeli foreman," *Personnel Psychology*, 23 (1970), pp.169-172.

72. Sadler, P.J. "Leadership Style, Confidence in Management, and Job Satisfaction," *Journal of Applied Behavioural Science*, 6 (1970), pp.3-19.

73. Tosi, H. "A Re-Examination of Personality as a determinant of the effects of Participation," *Personnel Psychology*, 23 (1970), pp.91-99.

74. Katzell, R.A., Miller, C.E., Rotter, N.G., and Vinet, T.G. "Effects of Leadership and other Inputs on Group Processes and Outputs," *Journal of Social Psychology*, 80, (1970), pp.157-169.

75. W.J. Reddin, *Managerial Effectiveness*, McGraw-Hill, New York, 1970.

76. R.J. House, "A Path-Goal Theory of Leader Effectiveness," *Administrative Science Quarterly*, September 1971, pp.321-338, and R.J. House and T.R.Mitchel, "Path-Goal Theory of Leadership," *Journal of Contemporary Business*, Autumn, 1974, p.86.

77. Misumi, J. "The Validation of Conceptional Model of Leadership Partners," Institute of Group Dynamics, Kyushu University, Japan, 1972.

78. Wexley, K.N., Singh, J.P. and Yukl, G.A. "Subordinate Personality as Moderator of the Effects of Participation in three types of Appraisal Interviews," *Journal of Applied Psychology*, 58 (1973), pp.54-59.

79. Brunson, R.W. and Wickhert, F.R. "The Empirical Investigation at the Contingency Theory within a Conglomerate," Paper Presented at the American Psychological Association, 1973.

80. V.H. Vroom and P.W. Yetton, *Leadership and Decision-Making*, University of Pittsburgh Press, Pittsburgh, 1973.

81. Nitish De, "Dilemmas of Indian Managers," *Management in Government*, July-September 1974.

82. Kakar, S., *Personality and Authority in Work*, Somaiya Publications, Bombay, 1974. p.17, p.100.

83. Elhance, D.N. and Agarwal, R.D. "Delegation of Authority," *Lok Udyog*, 6 (1973).

84. R.Rangaswamy and D.Helmick, "A Comparative Study of Indian and American Executives' Leadership Styles," *Indian Administrative and Management Review*, July-September 1976.

85. Sinha J.B.P. "The Authoritative Leadership: A Style of Effective Management," *Indian Journal of Industrial Relations*, 11 (1976), pp.381-389.

86. Kumar, Usha and Singh, K.K. "The Inter-Personal Construct System of the Indian Manager: A determinant of Organizational Behaviour," *Indian Journal of Psychology*, 51 (1976), 275-278, (p.288).

87. Lokhande M.R. and Singh S.N. "Leadership Patterns and Social Change," *Journal of the Council of Social Development*, Volume 7, No.1, March 1977, pp.14-19.

88. Verma, Jyoti. "A scale for measuring Leadership styles," A.N.S. Institute of social studies, Patna, 1977 (mimeographed).

89. P.M. Joseph and R.Kesavan, "A Comparative Study of Leader Behaviour in Public and Private Sectors in India," *Indian Manager*, April-June 1977.

90. Singh, A.P. and Das, G.S. "Management Style of Indian Manager: A profile," ASCI *Journal of Management*, September 1977.

91. Schuler, R.S. "Role Perception, Satisfaction and Performance Moderated by Organization Level and Participation in Decision-Making," *Academy of Management Journal*, 20, (1977), p.165.

92. S. Selvadurai, "Leadership in the Cooperatives: Some perceptions of Leaders," *Indian management*, July 1997, pp.40-45.

93. Sinha, T.N. and Sinha, J.B.P. "Styles of Leadership and

their effects on Group Productivity," A.N.S. Institute of Social Studies, Patna, 1977 (mimeographed).

94. B.L. Jaggi, "Management Leadership Styles in Indian Work Organizations," *Indian Manager*, April-June 1978.

95. Singh, P. "Leadership Process and its Impact on Productivity, Satisfaction and Work Commitment," *Decision*, Volume 6, 1979, pp.259-269.

96. H.K. Kalra "Leadership Styles of Executives in Indian Enterprises," unpublished Research Report, Punjab Agricultural University, Ludhiana, 1980.

97. Sinha, J.B.P., *The Nurturant Task-Behaviour*, Concept Publishing Company, New Delhi, 1980.

98. Habibullah, A.H.M. and Sinha, J.B.P. "Motivational Climate and Leadership Styles," *Vikalpa*, 5 (1980).

99. Jain, U. "Life Styles of Indian Managers: An Exploratory Study of the Images, Experiences and Impact of Collectors in their Districts," Unpublished Fellow Programme Dissertation, Indian Institute of Management, Ahmedabad, India, 1982.

100. Swarna Pratap and Srivastava, S.K. "Leadership Styles and Effectiveness: A comparative study," *Indian Journal of Industrial Relations*, Volume 21, No.1, July 1985, pp.94-97.

101. Muttayya, B.C. and Vijaya Kumar, S. "Leadership Styles, Perceived Need Satisfaction and Subjective Job Characteristics among Scientific Personnel," *Indian Journal of Industrial Relations*, Volume-21, No.2, October 1985, pp.173-182.

102. Ramakanth. J. "Attitudes of Managers in Public Enterprises," unpublished Thesis Submitted to Osmania University, Hyderabad, 1985.

103. R.P. Singh and Janak Pandey "Leadership Styles, Control Strategies and Personal Consequences," *Indian Journal of Industrial Relations*, Volume 22, No.1, July 1986, pp.41-51.

104. Ansari, M.A. "Need for Nurturant-Task Leaders in India: Some empirical evidence," *Management and Labour Studies*, 11,1, (1986), pp.26-36.

105. Neelam Varma, "A Test of Implicit Personality Theories of Leadership," *Indian Journal of Industrial Relations*, Volume 22, No.2, Oct, 1986, pp.189-198.

106. Hingar Asha, *Leadership Styles and Job Satisfaction*, Printwell Publishers, Jaipur, 1986.

107. Prabhakar Singh, "Nurturant Task and Participative Task Leaderships: The Effective Leader Behaviours for Indian Industries," *Indian Journal of Industrial Relations*, Volume.23, No.2, October 1987, pp.197-204.

108. Kapila, P.D., 'Leadership Styles in Public Sector', in 'Leadership and Managerial Effectiveness', Narayan, B. (Ed) *Janaki Prakashan*, New Delhi, 1987, pp. 49-54.

109. Rama Murthy, R. "Study on Leadership Styles in State Owned Enterprises," *Journal of General Management*, Volume 2, Winter, 1987, pp. 44-55.

110. .Lynn R. Anderson, "Towards a Two-Track Model of Leadership Training: Suggestions from Self-Monitoring Theory," *Small Group Research*, Vol.21, No.2, May 1990, pp.147-167.

111. R. Venkatapathy "Perception of Top Management Leadership Styles and Climate: A Study of Public and Private Executives," *Indian Journal of Industrial Relations*, Volume-25, No.3, January 1990.

112. Omer Bin Sayeed, "Conflict Management Styles: Relationship with Leadership Styles and Moderating Effect of Esteem for Coworker," *Indian Journal of Industrial Relations*, Vol.26, No.1, July 1990, pp.28-52.

113. Rama J. Joshi, "Managerial Effectiveness: As Perceived by Chief Executives," *Indian Journal of Industrial Relations*, Volume 27, No.1, July 1991, pp.69-78.

114. Rajinder Kaur, "Managerial Styles in the Public Sector,"

Indian Journal of Industrial Relations, Volume 28, No.4, April, 1993, pp.363-367.

115. N. Panchanatham, K. Rajendran, and K. K. Karuppiah, "A Study of Executive Leadership Styles and problem Solving Behaviour," *Indian Journal of Industrial Relations*, Volume-29, No.1, July 1993.

116. Manisha Agarwal and G.C. Agarwal, "Relationship of Middle Managers' Power Styles with their Participativeness at the Work Place," *Indian Journal of Industrial Relations*, Volume 30, No.3, January 1995, pp.278-288.

117. Subramanian and K. Sajjan Rao, "Attitudes of Union Leaders in Changing Realities- Direction Towards Greater Involvement," *Indian Journal of Industrial Relations*, Volume 32, No.4, April 1997. pp.409-422.

118. V. Ravichandran and D. Nagabrahmam, "Leadership in a Transitory Environment," *Indian Journal of Industrial Relations*, Volume 32, No.4, April 1997, pp.423-435.

119. Syed Vazith Hussain, "Leadership Styles in Small Scale Industries," *The Indian Journal of Commerce*, Vol.55, No.3, July-September 2002, pp.45-54.

4

Introduction to the Organisation

Company Profile

BEML Limited (formerly Bharat Earth Movers Limited) was established in May 1964 as a Public Sector Undertaking for manufacture of Rail Coaches & Spare Parts and Mining Equipment at its Bangalore Complex. The Company has partially disinvested and presently Government of India owns 54 percent of total equity and rest 46 percent is held by Public, Financial institutions, Foreign Institutional Investors, Banks and Employees.

During the financial year 2006-07, BEML achieved a sales turnover of US$ 650 mn (INR 2601 crores) and a pre tax profit of US$ 79 mn (INR 315 crores). The export earnings touched US$ 27.5 mn (INR 110 crores).

BEML Limited (BEML) conferred with Mini-Ratna Status and under the administrative control of Ministry of Defence, is a multi-technology company offering high-quality products for diverse sectors of economy such as coal, mining, steel, limestone, power, irrigation, construction, road building, aviation, defence, metro and railways. BEML is ranked as

"The Largest and Most Profitable Construction Equipment Company" by Construction World - NICMAR, 2007. It has emerged in the forefront of heavy engineering industry with a track record of growth and revenues for over four decades. For its innovative management practices the company has been awarded the "Golden Peacock Innovation Management Award". BEML has also been rated as "The Fourth Largest Wealth Creator in the Country" by *Dalal Street Magazine*. In keeping with the global technology trends, the company is setting up R&D Centre of Excellence for Research in Metro Rail System in Bangalore.

The main manufacturing facilities are located at Kolar Gold Fields, Mysore and Bangalore. These incorporate sophisticated facilities like CNC machines, hi-tech welding equipment and flexible manufacturing systems to turn out cutting-edge technology products. All three manufacturing facilities are certified for ISO 9001-2000.

BEML operates on three major business verticals for associated equipment manufacturing:

- Mining & Construction
- Defence
- Rail & Metro.

In addition to the above there are three services verticals:

- Technology Division for providing end-to-end engineering solutions
- Trading Division for dealing in non-company products
- International Business Division for export activities
- Technology Division for providing end-to-end engineering solutions
- Trading Division for dealing in non-company products

- International Business Division for export activities.

BEML has eight manufacturing units spread over four locations

Kolar Gold Fields (KGF) Complex (around 100 Km from Bangalore)

- Earth Moving Division
- Rail Coach Unit II
- Heavy Fabrication Unit
- Hydraulic & Powerline Division.

Mysore Complex (around 130 Km from Bangalore)

- Truck Division
- Engine Division

Bangalore Complex - Rail & Metro Division

Vignyan Industries, Tarikere (around 300 km from Bangalore) - Steel Castings

BEML's nationwide network of sales offices enables buyers with ready access to its wide range of products. Also, the full-fledged service centers and parts depots offer total equipment care, maintenance contracts and rehabilitation services.

Commitment to Quality

BEML Limited views Quality improvement as a business strategy and hence remains proactive in the areas of product and service quality. At BEML, a Corporate Quality Policy emphasizing Total Quality Management ensures that quality system adopted results in products, services and processes that meet stringent standards and requisite performance criteria. A separate Quality Department spearheads the thrust towards Total Quality Management.

All the manufacturing units of the company have been certified for ISO 9001-2000 Quality Management System Standards. The facilities include custom made test tracks to evaluate performance of the equipment. Also, the manufacturing divisions are augmented with test facilities available at its R&D / Technology Division. Laboratories at R&D, KGF and Mysore Complex are accredited to National Accreditation Board for Laboratories (NABL) covering Calibration of Flow, Pressure, Torque and Mechanical Measuring Instruments.

Well established vendor base is a key strength of BEML. Vendor assessment and development is a key component of the company's strategy for achieving Total Quality. Experienced professionals are positioned across India in 16 regions who are available at vendor's doorstep to facilitate them in improving the quality of products and services.

Quality Improvement initiatives required for both evolutionary and revolutionary improvements are in place. Concept of 5S, Kaizen and Quality Circles are practiced at grass root level. BEML is actively pursuing 'Six Sigma' methodologies to achieve break through in process / product improvements. In 2006, it has launched company-wide 'Six Sigma' movement and is currently spearheading the 'Second Wave' of Six Sigma initiatives.

'Quality Function Deployment' is actively pursued in the organization. Cross-functional teams routinely visit customer sites to capture 'Voice of Customer'. Such actions have resulted in incorporating a number of product improvements to fine tune product features on both in-house developed as well as collaborated products to suit specific customer requirements and operating conditions.

BEML actively promotes small group activities to encourage and enhance 'Quality Culture' at all levels. The small group activity teams regularly participate in regional and national level competition and have achieved recognition as meritorious performers and the eligibility to participate in international competition.

Joint Venture

BEML– MIDWEST JV COMPANY for Contract Mining.

BEML Midwest Limited, a Joint Venture Company was incorporated in April 2007 at Hyderabad, India to undertake Contract Mining along with Midwest Granite Private Limited, Hyderabad and Pt. Sumber Mitra Jaya, Jakarta, Indonesia as partners. The objective of the company is to successfully integrate the versatility, flexibility and freedom for cost effective operation also to quickly adopt instantaneous solutions.

Midwest Granite Private Limited, a Hyderabad based company is a leading player in the area of exploration, mining, processing and export of natural stones. With global marketing headquarters in US, it has a distribution network and operations spread across India, Sri Lanka, Turkey, Zimbabwe, Australia and Europe.

Pt. Sumber Mitra Jaya is an Indonesian Company with wide expertise in contract coal mining and production. It is the flagship of the Mitra Jaya Group and was founded in 1982 with headquarters at Jakarta, Indonesia.

5

Reflections of Leadership as Perceived by the Respondents

Leadership reveals the opinions of the employees in BEML in terms of their inner feelings about the meaning of leadership, leadership idealism, qualities of leaders which attracted them to recognize their leadership, benefits received from their leadership and the skills they have appreciated. This chapter fulfills the study of the view points of the employees of BEML on Leadership in their organisation.

It is evident from the Table 5.1 that 215 respondents felt that meaning for leadership is 'guiding' which accounts for 54 per cent, followed by 'controlling' is 167 (42 per cent), and 'protecting' by 144 persons (36 per cent). However, the commonly accepted meaning of 'influence' is preferred by 96 persons or 24 per cent of the sample. The least preferred meaning is 'loving' by 64 persons (16 per cent). This signifies that the guidance by the superior to the subordinates is a prime factor in the perception and expectation of the employees working in BEML.

Table 5.1
Leadership according to officers of BEML (N=399)

Ranks meaning	*Leadership responses*	*Number of (in Percentage)*	*Responses*
I	Guiding	215	54
II	Controlling	167	42
III	Protecting	144	36
IV	Influencing	96	24
V	Loving	64	16

Source: Compiled from field survey.

Table 5.2
Ideal Leader according to officers of BEML (N=399)

Ranks	*Ideal leader*	*Number of responses*	*Responses (In Percentage)*
I	Father	143	36
II	Mother	135	34
III	Boss (supervisor)	128	32
IV	Teacher (Guru)	120	30
V	Friend	80	20
VI	Religious Guru	72	18
VII	Spouse	56	14
VIII	Uncle	40	10
IX	Politician	24	6

Source: Compiled from field survey

Table 5.2 reveals that 143 employees (36 per cent) have chosen 'father' as the leader followed by 'mother' by 135 employees (34 per cent). 'Boss (supervisor)' was chosen by 128 employees (32 per cent) as the leader. In the ranking of the leader, 'teacher' occupying 4th position accounting for 30 per cent was chosen by 120 employees. 'Friend' was chosen by 80 employees (20 per cent) as the leader. Employees who have chosen 'religious guru' as their leader were 72 accounts for 18 per cent. 'Spouse' was chosen by 56 employees (14 per cent) as the leader. 'Uncle' was chosen by 40 employees (10 per cent) as the leader. The 'politician' is preferred to be recognized as a leader only by 24 or 6 per cent of employees. This is probably due to lack of personal contact of employees with politicians.

This signifies that in masculine societies father has a predominant role in playing the leadership role followed by mother.

Table 5.3
Benefits, qualities and skills (N=399)

Ranks		*Number of responses*	*Responses (In Percentage)*
1	*2*	*3*	*4*
	A. BENEFITS		
I	Knowledge	304	76
II	Moral support	243	61
III	Social status	119	29
IV	Promotion	97	24
V	Financial benefits	78	19
VI	Power	77	19
VII	Employment	73	18
	B. QUALITIES		
I	Self-confidence	283	71
II	Discipline	266	66
III	Courage	212	53
IV	Patience	189	47

(Contd...)

1	*2*	*3*	*4*
V	Kindness	160	40
VI	Justice	149	37
VII	Competitive spirit	132	33
VIII	Ambition	125	31
IX	Vision	121	30
X	Tolerance	112	28
XI	Forgiveness	102	25
XII	Perseverance	80	20
XIII	Spirituality	70	17
XIV	Compassion	56	14
XV	Humility	51	12
	C. SKILLS		
I	Hardwork	227	57
II	Decision making skills	225	56
III	Art of communication	226	56
IV	Administrative skills	188	47
V	Art of listening	181	45
VI	Art of living	125	31
VII	Tact and diplomacy	120	30
VIII	Inspirational power	88	22
IX	Humour	62	15

Source: Compiled from field survey

Table 5.3 reveals that about 76 per cent or 304 employees out of 399 have expressed that the major contribution of their leaders is knowledge. Moral support has occupied second place as 243 (61 per cent) out of 399 employees opted for it. Other aspects like power, financial benefits, employment, promotion and social status have been negligible in the options of all cadres of employees.

The major qualities that have drawn the attention of employees in their leaders are self-confidence and discipline, which have accounted for 283 or 71 per cent and 266 or 66 per cent respectively. Other qualities like ambition, courage, perseverance, patience, tolerance, humility, compassion, competitive spirit, spirituality, justice, forgiveness, kindness and vision have not been considered as important factors by the employees.

The significant skills among the leaders of employees in BEML cover industry and communication accounting for 227 out of 339 or 57 per cent and 226 out of 339 or 56 per cent respectively. The other skills like decision making skills, art of listening, art of living, administrative skills, tact and diplomacy, inspirational power and humour have not attracted the attention by the employees.

Table 5.4

Some qualities are also essential to become a leader (N=399)

Ranks	*Qualities*	*Number of responses*	*Responses (In Percentage)*
I	Pride	181	45
II	Self-interest	54	13
III	Ego	51	12
III	Cunningness	48	12
IV	Harshness	40	10
IV	Anger	40	10
V	Envy	18	4
VI	Arrogance	16	4
VII	Greed	12	3
VIII	Pomp	5	1
IX	Hypocrisy	3	1

Source: Compiled from field survey

Table 5.4 reveals that 181 employees (45 per cent) and 54 employees (13 per cent) have expressed that the qualities like the pride and self-interest are also essential for an effective leader.

Table 5.5
Qualities which do not go with effective Leadership (N=399)

Ranks	*Qualities*	*Number of responses*	*Responses (In Percentage)*
I	Insincerity	156	39
II	Indifference	130	32
III	Laziness	111	27
IV	Ignorance	90	22
VI	Timidity	64	16
VIII	Pessimism	48	12

Source: Compiled from field survey.

Table 5.5 reveals that the qualities like insincerity and indifference are not appreciated by the employees, among their leaders accounting for 156 out of 399 or 39 per cent and 130 out of 399 or 32 per cent respectively. Though the above mentioned (in Table 5.5) traits or aspects do not go with effective acceptable leadership, in some cases people with these traits function as leaders. In a given socio-cultural situation individuals predominantly endowed with these traits function as Leaders even though people in a given situation know the bad or undesirable qualities in them who dominate as functional leaders.

Leadership Styles: Self Perception

The behaviour of human beings much more in the capacity of leaders affects not only the behaviour and performance of others but also of the organisations. However, the behaviour of the leaders is closely related to the perceptions and attitudes they maintain relating to their purposes, roles and functions. The perceptions are consolidated from their self perceptions and their perceptions towards their own leaders who influenced or guided their missions and methods. Thus the performance of the leaders is the outcome of the approaches they adopt in their jobs which are the resultant effects of their own perceptions about their own leaders. The nature of person, without any exception to a leader is to emulate and imitate their own ideal personalities. What are the perceptions of different employees in different grades in their leadership role relating to the inspiration and influence they have drawn from their predecessors. The analysis of the employees in several grades i.e., Higher level managers, Middle level managers and Lower level managers, forms the subject matter of this chapter. Here may briefly look into an individual self perception influences his interactions with his super-ordinates and subordinates. Often Leaders style of functioning depends on the people with whom he interacts and the task entrusted with. Further as discussed below there are other dimensions which influence a leader is perceived by superior or subordinate groups.

The organisational effectiveness depends on the leadership effectiveness. Leadership effectiveness varies with the socio-economic organizational position variables. Besides this, the styles like authoritarian, participative, bureaucratic, task-orientation and nurturant of the leaders influence the followers and their performance resulting in overall efficiency of the people and effectiveness of the organisation. The organisation positions of BEML included for the study cover Higher level managers, Middle level managers and Lower level managers. The socio-economic organizational position variables include viz., designation, age, experience, education and economic status.

In BEML the total sample of the study was 399 officers belonging to three functional levels. Being at the extreme levels in the hierarchy the subordinates' perception has not been taken into account in the case of Higher Level Managers and the self perception is ignored in the case of Lower Level Managers, they being in the bottom of the hierarchy.

Thus, the leader's self perception reveals about the styles of Higher Level Managers, and Middle Level Managers, of BEML. Scores on five leadership styles were computed from leader's evaluation of ones own style.

The correlations among selected socio-economic and organizational position variables were computed. Following this, the correlations of socio-economic and organizational position variables with leadership styles were computed. In addition, correlations were computed among five leadership styles.

In this chapter the presentation and discussion of the data pertains to the following:

I. Inter-correlation of SEOP variables of officers in BEML viz., Higher level managers, Middle level managers and Lower level managers.

II. Relationship of SEOP variables with leadership styles of officers in BEML viz., Higher level managers and Middle level managers.

III. Inter-correlation of leadership styles of officers in BEML viz., Higher level managers and Middle level managers.

I. Inter-Correlation of SEOP Variables

A. *Higher Level Managers of BEML*

For the inter-correlation, the degree of freedom (df) is N-2. In BEML, Higher Level Managers stood 48, where N=48, the df=48-2=46. For 46 df the entries at 0.01 and 0.05 by linear interpolation are 0.372 and 0.288 respectively (for 3 decimals). The correlation values with two stars are significant at 0.01 level and those with one star is significant at 0.05 level.

Table 6.1
Inter-correlations among SEOP Variables for Higher Level Managers of BEML (N=48)

S. No.	*SEOP Variables*	*Designation*	*Age*	*Experi-ence*	*Educa-tion*	*Economic Status*
1	Designation		**0.470	**0.737	0.127	*-0.290
2	Age			**0.652	0.092	**-0.400
3	Experience				0.228	*-0.320
4	Education					0.000
5	Economic Status					

Source: Compiled from field survey

Table 6.1 presents the inter-correlations among socio-economic and organizational position variables viz., designation, age, experience, education, and economic status for Higher Level Managers of Bharath Earth Movers Limited.

The variable 'designation' was significantly and positively correlated with 'age'(r=0.470, P<0.01) indicating that higher the designation, greater the age. 'designation' was also significantly and positively correlated with 'experience' (r=0.737, P<0.01) signifying that the designation increases with the increase in the 'experience'. 'designation' was also significantly but negatively correlated with 'economic status' (r= -0.290, P<0.05) signifying that the economic status decreases with the increase in the 'designation'.

The variable 'age' was significantly and positively correlated with 'experience'(r=0.652, P<0.01) indicating that higher the age, greater the experience. 'age' was also significantly but negatively correlated with 'economic status' (r= -0.400, P<0.01) signifying that the economic status decreases with the increase in the 'age'.

The variable 'experience' was significantly but negatively correlated with 'economic status' (r= -0.320, P<0.05) signifying that the economic status decreases with the increase in the 'experience'.

None of the other socio-economic and organizational position variables, however, were found not to be significantly inter-correlated. They are rather, independent of each other.

Hence, the hypothesis of "there is no significant inter-relationship among the socio-economic and organizational position variables of employees in Bharath Earth Movers Limited" is rejected in the case of designation vs age; designation vs experience and designation vs economic status; age vs experience and age vs economic status; experience vs economic status and is accepted in all other cases.

B. *Middle Level Managers of BEML*

For the inter-correlation, the degree of freedom (df) is N-2. In BEML, Middle Level Managers stood 136, where N=136, the df=136-2=134. For 134 df the entries at 0.01 and 0.05 by linear interpolation are 0.254 and 0.195 respectively (for 3 decimals). The correlation values with two stars are significant at 0.01 level and those with one star is significant at 0.05 level.

Table 6.2
Inter-correlations among SEOP Variables for Middle Level Managers of BEML (N=136)

S. No.	*SEOP Variables*	*Designation*	*Age*	*Experi-ence*	*Educa-tion*	*Economic Status*
1	Designation		**0.507	**0.458	0.074	0.006
2	Age			**0.915	0.045	*0.198
3	Experience				-0.08	0.173
4	Education					0.01
5	Economic Status					

Source: Compiled from field survey

Table 6.2 presents the inter-correlations among socio-economic and organizational position variables viz., designation, age, experience, education and economic status for Middle Level Managers of Bharath Earth Movers Limited.

The variable 'designation' was significantly and positively correlated with 'age'(r=0.507, P<0.01) indicating that higher the designation, greater the age. 'designation' was also significantly and positively correlated with 'experience' (r=0.458, P<0.01) signifying that the designation increases with the increase in the 'experience'.

The variable 'age' was significantly and positively correlated with 'experience'(r=0.916, P<0.01) indicating that higher the age, greater the experience. 'age' was also significantly and positively correlated with 'economic status' (r= 0.198, P<0.05) signifying that the economic status increases with the increase in the 'age'.

None of the other socioeconomic and organizational position variables, however, were found not to be significantly inter-correlated. They are rather, independent of each other.

Hence, the hypothesis of "there is no significant inter relationship among socio-economic and organizational position variables of employees in Bharath Earth Movers Limited" is rejected in the case of designation vs age; designation vs experience; age vs experience and age vs economic status and is accepted in all other cases.

C. Lower Level Managers of BEML

For the inter-correlation, the degree of freedom (df) is N-2. In BEML, Lower Level Managers stood 215, where N=215, the df=215-2=213. For 213 df the entries at 0.01 and 0.05 by linear interpolation are 0.254 and 0.195 respectively (for 3 decimals). The correlation values with two stars are significant at 0.01 level and those with one star is significant at 0.05 level.

Table 6.3
Inter-correlations among SEOP Variables for Lower Level Managers of BEML (N=215)

S. No.	SEOP Variables	Designation	Age	Experience	Education	Economic Status
1	Designation		0.097	-0.030	**0.350	0.156
2	Age			**0.877	0.132	-0.020
3	Experience				0.013	-0.020
4	Education					0.165
5	Economic Status					

Source: Compiled from field survey

Table 6.3 presents the inter-correlations among socio-economic and organizational position variables viz., designation, age, experience, education and economic status for Lower Level Managers of Bharath Earth Movers Limited.

The variable 'designation' was significantly and positively correlated with 'education' ($r=0.350$, $P<0.01$) indicating that higher the designation, greater the education.

The variable 'age' was significantly and positively correlated with 'experience'($r=0.877$, $P<0.01$) indicating that higher the age, greater the experience.

None of the other socio-economic and organizational position variables, however, were found not to be significantly inter-correlated. They are rather, independent of each other.

Hence, the hypothesis of "there is no significant inter relationship among socio-economic and organizational position variables of employees in Bharath Earth Movers Limited" is rejected in the case of designation vs education and age vs experience and is accepted in all other cases.

II. Inter-Correlation Between SEOP Variables and Leadership Styles

Table 6.4
Inter-correlation between SEOP variables and Leadership Styles for Higher Level Managers (N=48)

		Leadership Styles				
S. No.	*SEOP Variables*	*Authori-tarian*	*Partic-ipative*	*Burea-ucratic*	*Task-orientation*	*Nurturant*
1	Designation	-0.161	*0.336	0.237	**0.376	**0.457
2	Age	-0.151	-0.200	0.045	0.106	0.091
3	Experience	*-0.302	0.078	0.062	0.007	0.086
4	Education	-0.137	0.174	-0.050	0.237	0.074
5	Economic Status	0.021	0.031	-0.150	-0.090	-0.060

Source: Compiled from field survey

Table 6.4 presents the inter-correlation between socio-economic and organizational position variables and five leadership styles viz., authoritarian, participative, bureaucratic, task-orientation and nurturant for Higher Level Managers of Bharath Earth Movers Limited.

'designation' was correlated significantly and positively with 'pariticpative' style (r= 0.336, P<0.05), 'task-orientation' style (r= 0.376, P<0.01) and 'nurturant' style(r= 0.457, P<0.01) indicating that 'participative', 'task-orientation' and 'nurturant' styles increases with the increase of 'designation'.

The correlation between 'experience' and 'authoritarian' style of leadership was found to be significantly negative(r= -0.302, P<0.05) indicating that the 'authoritarian' style increases with the decrease of 'experience'.

None of the other socio-economic and organizational position variables, however, were found not to be significantly correlated with leadership styles.

Hence, the hypothesis of "there is no significant relationship between socio-economic and organizational position variables and leadership styles of employees in Bharath Earth Movers Limited" is rejected in the case of 'designation' vs 'participative', 'designation' vs 'task-orientation', 'designation' vs 'nurturant', 'experience' vs 'authoritarian', and is accepted in all other cases.

Table 6.5

Inter-correlation between SEOP variables and Leadership Styles for Middle Level Managers (N=136)

		Leadership Styles				
S. No.	*SEOP Variables*	*Authori-tarian*	*Partic-ipative*	*Burea-ucratic*	*Task-orientation*	*Nurturant*
1	Designation	-0.042	0.037	-0.150	-0.100	0.062
2	Age	0.111	-0.050	-0.040	-0.100	0.109
3	Experience	0.132	-0.050	-0.050	-0.080	0.182
4	Education	-0.072	-0.010	-0.190	-0.050	-0.020
5	Economic Status	0.141	-0.050	-0.100	-0.000	0.029

Source: Compiled from field survey

Table 6.5 presents the inter-correlation between socio-economic and organizational position variables and five leadership styles viz., authoritarian, participative, bureaucratic, task-orientation and nurturant for Middle Level Managers of Bharath Earth Movers Limited.

No socio-economic and organizational position variables were found not to be significantly correlated with leadership styles.

Hence, the hypothesis of "there is no significant relationship between socio-economic and organizational position variables and leadership styles of employees in Bharath Earth Movers Limited" is accepted.

III. Inter-Correlation of Leadership Styles

Table 6.6
Inter-correlation of Leadership Styles for Higher Level Managers (N=48)

Leadership Styles	*Authori-tarian*	*Partic-ipative*	*Burea-ucratic*	*Task-or ientation*	*Nurturant*
Authoritarian		0.167	0.086	0.078	0.212
Participative			-0.02	0.218	*0.327
Bureaucratic				**0.436	0.275
Task-orientation					**0.731
Nurturant					

Source: Compiled from field survey.

Table 6.6 presents the inter-corrélations among leadership styles for Higher Level Managers of Bharath Earth Movers Limited.

The 'participative' style was correlated significantly and positively with 'nurturant' style($r=0.327$, $P<0.05$) indicating that 'nurturant' styles increases with the increase of 'participative' style

The 'bureaucratic' style was correlated significantly and positively with 'task-orientation' style($r=0.436$, $P<0.01$) indicating that 'bureaucratic' style increases with the increase of 'task-orientation' style.

The 'task-orientation' style was correlated significantly and positively with 'nurturant' style($r=0.731$, $P<0.01$) indicating that 'nurturant' styles increases with the increase of 'task-orientation' style.

Hence, the hypothesis of "there is no significant relationship among leadership styles of employees in Bharath Earth Movers Limited" is rejected in the case of 'participative' vs 'nurturant', 'bureaucratic' vs 'task-orientation', and 'task-orientation' vs 'nurturant' styles and is accepted in all other cases.

Table 6.7
Inter-correlation of Leadership Styles for Middle Level Managers (N=136)

Leadership Styles	*Authori-tarian*	*Partic-ipative*	*Burea-ucratic*	*Task-or ientation*	*Nurturant*
Authoritarian		-0.080	**0.293	*0.223	0.126
Participative			-0.030	**0.335	**0.418
Bureaucratic				0.135	0.055
Task-orientation					**0.594
Nurturant					

Source: Compiled from field survey.

Table 6.7 presents the inter-correlations among leadership styles for Middle Level Managers of Bharath Earth Movers Limited.

The 'authoritarian' style was correlated significantly and positively with 'bureaucratic' style(r=0.293, P<0.01) and 'task-orientation' style(r=0.223, P<0.05) indicating that 'bureaucratic' and 'task-orientation' styles increases with the increase of 'authoritarian' style.

The 'participative' style was correlated significantly and positively with 'task-orientation' style(r=0.335, P<0.01) and 'nurturant' style(r=0.418, P<0.01) indicating that 'task-orientation' and 'nurturant' style increases with the increase of 'participative' style.

The 'task-orientation' style was correlated significantly and positively with 'nurturant' style(r=0.594, P<0.01) indicating that 'nurturant' styles increases with the increase of 'task-orientation' style.

Hence, the hypothesis of "there is no significant relationship among leadership styles of employees in Bharath Earth Movers Limited" is rejected in the case of 'authoritarian' vs 'bureaucratic', 'authoritarian' vs 'task-orientation' 'participative' vs 'task-orientation', 'participative' vs 'nurturant' and 'task-orientation' vs 'nurturant' styles and is accepted in all other cases.

Leadership Styles: Subordinates Perception

Here we may focus on subordinates perception of leadership styles. The organisational effectiveness and leadership effectiveness are well-knit to each other. In other words the performance of the people is based on their perceptions about themselves, their superiors and subordinates. These perceptions decide the quality of interpersonal relations among the managers in their leadership role while dealing with their subordinates. Similarly the subordinates accept their leaders basing on the styles they adopt.

This chapter presents the leadership styles perceived by subordinates viz., Middle Level Managers and Lower Level Managers of BEML.

The correlations of socio-economic and organizational position variables with leadership styles were computed. Following this, correlations were computed among five leadership styles viz., authoritarian, participative, bureaucratic, task-orientation and nurturant.

In this chapter the presentation and discussion of the data pertains to the following:

I. Relationship of SEOP variables with leadership styles for officers of BEML viz., Middle Level Managers and Lower Level Managers.

II. Inter-correlation of leadership styles for officers of BEML viz., Middle Level Managers and Lower Level Managers.

I. Inter-Correlation Between SEOP Variables and Leadership Styles

Table 7.1

Inter-correlation between SEOP variables and Leadership Styles of Middle Level Managers (N=136)

		Leadership Styles				
S. No.	*SEOP Variables*	*Authoritarian*	*Participative*	*Bureaucratic*	*Task-orientation*	*Nurturant*
1	Designation	-0.059	0.091	-0.100	0.023	0.122
2	Age	0.078	*0.208	-0.020	0.069	0.188
3	Experience	0.119	0.163	-0.060	0.089	0.175
4	Education	0.038	-0.020	-0.060	-0.360	*-0.250
5	Economic Status	-0.094	0.189	-0.000	0.098	0.133

Source: Compiled from field survey.

Table 7.1 presents the inter-correlation between socio-economic and organizational position variables and five leadership styles of Middle Level Managers of Bharath Earth Movers Limited.

The correlation between 'age' and 'participative' style of leadership was found to be significantly positive($r= 0.208$, $P<0.05$) indicating that the 'participative' style increases with the increase of 'age'.

The correlation between 'education' and 'nurturant' style of leadership was found to be significantly negative($r= -0.250$, $P<0.05$) indicating that the 'task-orientation' style decreases with the increase of 'education'.

None of the other socio-economic and organisational position variables, however, were found not to be significantly correlated with leadership styles.

Hence, the hypothesis of "there is no significant relationship between socio-economic and organisational position variables and leadership styles of employees in Bharath Earth Movers Limited" is rejected in the case of 'age' vs 'participative' and 'education' vs 'nurturant' style and is accepted in all other cases.

Table 7.2

Inter-correlation between SEOP variables and Leadership Styles of Lower Level Managers (N=215)

		Leadership Styles				
S. No.	*SEOP Variables*	*Authori- tarian*	*Partic- ipative*	*Burea- ucratic*	*Task-or ientation*	*Nurturant*
1	Designation	-0.020	-0.030	*0.228	-0.060	0.124
2	Age	-0.037	-0.030	-0.030	-0.060	0.030
3	Experience	-0.008	-0.030	0.059	-0.060	0.006
4	Education	0.0172	-0.150	-0.070	0.010	0.024
5	Economic Status	-0.078	-0.020	-0.110	-0.070	0.020

Source: Compiled from field survey.

Table 7.2 presents the inter-correlation between socio-economic and organizational position variables and five leadership styles of Senior Managers of Bharath Earth Movers Limited.

The correlation between 'designation' and 'bureaucratic' style of leadership was found to be significantly positive($r = 0.228$, $P<0.05$) indicating that the 'bureaucratic' style increases with the increase of 'designation'.

None of the other socio-economic and organisational position variables, however, were found not to be significantly correlated with leadership styles.

Hence, the hypothesis of "there is no significant relationship between socioeconomic and organisational position variables and leadership styles of employees in Bharath Earth Movers Limited" is rejected in the case of 'designation' vs 'bureaucratic' and is accepted in all other cases.

II. Inter-Correlation of Leadership Styles

Table 7.3
Inter-correlation of Leadership Styles of Middle Level Managers (N=136)

Leadership Styles	*Authoritarian*	*Participative*	*Bureaucratic*	*Task-orientation*	*Nurturant*
Authoritarian		**-0.270	0.032	**-0.280	**-0.240
Participative			**0.536	**0.699	**0.764
Bureaucratic				**0.414	**0.448
Task-orientation					**0.815
Nurturant					

Source: Compiled from field survey

Table 7.3 presents the inter-correlations among leadership styles of Middle Level Managers of Bharath Earth Movers Limited.

The 'authoritarian' style was correlated significantly and negatively with 'participative' style($r=-0.270$, $P<0.01$), 'task-orientation' style($r=-0.280$, $P<0.01$) and with 'nurturant' style($r=-0.240$, $P<0.01$) indicating that 'participative', 'task-orientation' and 'nurturant' styles increases with the decrease of 'authoritarian' style.

The 'participative' style was correlated significantly and positively with 'bureaucratic' style($r=0.536$, $P<0.01$), 'task-orientation' style($r=0.699$, $P<0.01$) and with 'nurturant' style($r=0.764$, $P<0.01$) indicating that 'bureaucratic', 'task-orientation' and 'nurturant' styles increases with the increase of 'participative' style.

The 'bureaucratic' style was correlated significantly and positively with 'task-orientation' style(r=0.414, P<0.01) and with 'nurturant' style(r=0.448, P<0.01) indicating that 'task-orientation' and 'nurturant' styles increases with the increase of 'bureaucratic' style.

The 'task-orientation' style was correlated significantly and positively with 'nurturant' style(r=0.815, P<0.01) indicating that 'nurturant' styles increases with the increase of 'task-orientation' style.

Hence, the hypothesis of "there is no significant relationship among leadership styles of employees in Bharath Earth Movers Limited" is rejected in the case of 'authoritarian' vs 'participative', 'authoritarian' vs 'task-orientation', 'authoritarian' vs 'nurturant', 'participative vs 'bureaucratic', 'participative' vs 'task-orientation', 'participative' vs 'nurturant', 'bureaucratic' vs 'task-orientation', 'bureaucratic' vs 'nurturant', and 'task-orientation' vs 'nurturant' and is accepted in the case of authoritarian vs bureaucratic style.

Table 7.4
Inter-correlation of Leadership Styles of Lower Level Managers (N=215)

Leadership Styles	*Authoritarian*	*Participative*	*Bureaucratic*	*Task-orientation*	*Nurturant*
Authoritarian		-0.150	*0.221	-0.080	*-0.240
Participative			**0.264	**0.423	**0.669
Bureaucratic				*0.228	**0.288
Task-orientation					**0.528
Nurturant					

Source: Compiled from field survey.

Table 7.4 presents the inter-correlations among leadership styles of Lower Level Managers of Bharath Earth Movers Limited.

The 'authoritarian' style was correlated significantly and positively with 'bureaucratic' style (r=0.221, P<0.05), indicating that 'bureaucratic' style increases with the increase of 'authoritarian' style. 'authoritarian'. style was also correlated significantly but negatively with 'nurturant' style(r=-0.240, P<0.05), indicating that 'nurturant' style increases with the decrease of 'authoritarian' style.

The 'participative' style was correlated significantly and positively with 'bureaucratic' style (r=0.264, P<0.01), 'task-orientation' style(r=0.423, P<0.01) and with 'nurturant' style(r=0.669, P<0.01) indicating that 'bureaucratic', 'task-orientation' and 'nurturant' styles increases with the increase of 'participative' style.

The 'bureaucratic' style was correlated significantly and positively with 'task-orientation' style (r=0.228, P<0.01) and with 'nurturant' style (r=0.288, P<0.01) indicating that 'task-orientation' and 'nurturant' styles increases with the increase of 'bureaucratic' style.

The 'task-orientation' style was correlated significantly and positively with 'nurturant' style(r=0.528, P<0.01) indicating that 'nurturant' styles increases with the increase of 'task-orientation' style.

Hence, the hypothesis of "there is no significant relationship among leadership styles of employees in Bharath Earth Movers Limited" is rejected in the case of 'authoritarian' vs 'bureaucratic', 'authoritarian' vs 'nurturant', 'participative vs 'bureaucratic', 'participative' vs 'task-orientation', 'participative' vs 'nurturant', 'bureaucratic' vs 'task-orientation', 'bureaucratic' vs 'nurturant', and 'task-orientation' vs 'nurturant' and is accepted in all other cases.

6

Summary of Findings and Suggestions

The summary of the findings of the study is presented in the following paragraphs.

To lead means to guide, direct and precede. Leadership is a process of influencing the behaviour, beliefs and feelings of the members of a group. The functions of leadership however, cover wide range of activities like coordinating, decision-making, policymaking, group representing, controlling, arbitrating, etc. Leadership, not being a single phenomenon, is affected by many variables and involves with several skills like technical, human, conceptual, designing, creative, communicative and decision making. The main aspect of influencing people by a leader is the power, which has many sources. The leadership effectiveness covers the personality of leader, past experience, expectations of superiors, the characteristics of subordinates', the requirements of the task, and the organisational climate and policies.

Twentieth century has witnessed several theories on leadership which is a complex concept having a bearing on motivation, morale, organizational climate, human relations, and communication. The ability to influence people in a group is indispensable in organizations. Beginning with scientific management the evolutionary process of leadership can be traced with three theories viz., trait theory, behavioural theory and contingency theory. The trait theory has been put to rigorous research by Byrd, Jennings, Gheselli, Stogdill etc., and resulted in the development of behavioral theory. Likert's system 4 theory, McGregor x and y theory, Continuum theory of Tannenbaum and Schmidt, etc. has opened new vistas on the behavioural dimensions of leadership. The confusion and controversy of trait and behavioural theories have given way to the contingency models of leadership like Fiedler's contingency model, Vroom and Yetton contingency model, path goal theory, life cycle theory, tri-dimensional model, learning model, etc.

A. Findings

I. The following are the major findings of the concepts and constructs of leadership.

1. The analysis relating to the concepts and constructs of leadership basing on the perceptions of 399 employees of BEML reveals that 'guiding' is the preferred meaning for majority of the respondents followed by controlling, protecting, influencing and loving.
2. The analysis reveals that 'father' was preferred as leader by majority followed by mother, boss (supervisor), teacher, friend, religious guru, spouse, uncle and politician.
3. The opinions expressed by employees about the benefits, knowledge was preferred by majority followed by moral support, social status, promotion, financial benefits, power and employment. 'self-confidence' was preferred by majority among the qualities followed by

discipline, courage, patience, kindness, justice, competitive spirit, ambition, vision, tolerance, forgiveness, perseverance, spirituality, compassion and humility. Hardwork was preferred by majority followed by decision making, communication, administration, listening, art of living, tact, diplomacy, inspirational power and humour in the case of skills.

4. The analysis reveals that majority of employees of BEML, expressed that the qualities like the pride and self-interest are also essential for an effective leader.

5. The employees of BEML do not appreciate the qualities like insincerity and indifference among leaders.

II. The following are the major findings of leader's self perception.

1. In BEML, at Higher Level Managers, a significant inter relationship among socio-economic organizational position variables is found in the case of designation vs age, designation vs experience, designation vs economic status, age vs experience, age vs economic status and experience vs economic status. No significant inter relationship is found among other socio-economic organizational position variables.

2. In BEML, at Middle Level Managers, a significant inter relationship among socio-economic organizational position variables is found in the case of designation vs age, designation vs experience, age vs experience and age vs economic status. No significant inter relationship is found among other socio-economic organizational position variables.

3. In BEML, at Lower Level Managers, a significant inter-relationship among socio-economic organizational position variables is found in the case of designation vs education and age vs experience. No significant inter

relationship is found among other socio-economic organizational position variables.

4. In BEML, at Higher Level Managers, a significant relationship between socio-economic organizational position variables and leadership styles as perceived by leaders themselves is found in the case of 'designation' vs 'participative', 'designation' vs 'task-orientation' 'designation' vs 'nurturant', 'experience' vs 'authoritarian' styles. No significant relationship is found between other socio-economic organizational position variables and leadership styles.
5. In BEML, at Middle Level Managers, no significant relationship is found between other socio-economic organizational position variables and leadership styles.
6. In BEML, at Higher Level Managers, a significant inter relationship among leadership styles is found in the case of 'participative' vs 'nurturant', 'bureaucratic' vs 'task-orientation' and 'task-orientation' vs 'nurturant' styles. No significant inter relationship is found among other leadership styles.
7. In BEML, at Middle Level Managers, a significant inter relationship among leadership styles is found in the case of 'authoritarian' vs 'bureaucratic', 'authoritarian' vs 'task-orientation' 'participative' vs 'task-orientation', 'participative' vs 'nurturant' and 'task-orientation' vs 'nurturant' styles. No significant inter relationship is found among other leadership styles.

III The following are the major findings of subordinate's perception on superior style.

1. In BEML, at Middle Level Managers, a significant relationship between socio-economic organizational position variables and leadership styles is found in the case of 'age' vs 'participative' and 'education' vs

'nurturant' style. No significant relationship is found between other socio-economic organizational position variables and leadership styles.

2. In BEML, at Lower Level Managers, a significant relationship between socio-economic organizational position variables and leadership styles is found in the case of 'designation' vs 'bureaucratic' style. No significant relationship is found between other socio-economic organizational position variables and leadership styles.
3. In BEML, at Middle Level Managers, a significant inter relationship among leadership styles is found in the case of 'authoritarian' vs 'participative', 'authoritarian' vs 'task-orientation', 'authoritarian' vs 'nurturant', 'participative vs 'bureaucratic', 'participative' vs 'task-orientation', 'participative' vs 'nurturant', 'bureaucratic' vs 'task-orientation', 'bureaucratic' vs 'nurturant', and 'task-orientation' vs 'nurturant'. No significant inter-relationship is found among other leadership styles.
4. In BEML, at Lower Level Managers, a significant inter relationship among leadership styles is found in the case of 'authoritarian' vs 'bureaucratic', 'authoritarian' vs 'nurturant', 'participative vs 'bureaucratic', 'participative' vs 'task-orientation', 'participative' vs 'nurturant', 'bureaucratic' vs 'task-orientation', 'bureaucratic' vs 'nurturant', and 'task-orientation' vs 'nurturant'. No significant inter relationship is found among other leadership styles.

B. Suggestions

Leadership is the most pervasive activity touching every facet of human existence. However, leadership is affected by innumerable variables creating an incomprehensive picture. Thus, it had become very difficult to adopt a particular concept, construct, and style. Nevertheless, the poor leadership, inappropriate to the organisational context would definitely create an environment of poor relationships and lower turnover. Owing to these complexities the major suggestion that can be made is that the knowledge and practice of leadership is to be taught preferably from lower levels of education.

Irrespective of the sector, activity and operation the leadership is to be strengthened so as to achieve the desired results. However, there cannot be uniform package of leadership that can be suggested to deal with all the organisational situations due to their wide variance. Organisations should also create congenial environment wherein the leader realises his/her role and discharge responsibility to fulfill the individual as well as organisational goals.

C. Conclusions

1. The overall analysis relating to the concepts and constructs of leadership basing on the perceptions of 399 employees reveals that the 'guiding' is the preferred meaning for majority of the respondents over other factors like 'controlling', 'protecting', 'influencing' and 'loving'.

2. Further 'father' was preferred as leader by majority rather than the 'mother', 'teacher', and so on.

3. The opinions expressed by the employees about the benefits, qualities, skills, 'knowledge' was preferred by majority followed by 'moral support', 'friendship' and the like.

4. The employees were skewed towards 'self-confidence' as against 'hard work' in the case of qualities and skills respectively over other variables.

5. The analysis of self perception in BEML reveals that at officers' level, the dominant style is nurturant, followed by task-orientation, participative, bureaucratic and authoritative styles.

6. The analysis of subordinates perception on superior styles, reveals that at officers level the dominant style is 'nurturant', followed by 'task-orientation', 'bureaucratic', 'participative' and 'authoritarian' styles.

7. At officers' level, in both self-perception as well as in subordinates' perception on superior styles a significant relationship between certain SEOP variables and leadership styles can be seen.

Appendix-1

SCHEDULES FOR LEADERSHIP

These schedules are designed to understand the basic issues of Leadership, in which every individual involves either as a Leader or led or both. Your responses will be kept confidential and individual identity will not be revealed.

SCHEDULE-I

1. Identification

1.1 Name : [No compulsion to mention]

1.2 Age :

1.3 Designation :

1.4 Experience (in years) :

1.5 Educational qualifications:

1.6 Economic background: Lower Middle Class ( )

Middle Class ( )

Upper Class ( )

SCHEDULE-II

2. Leadership (concept)

2.1. Please mention your meaning to leadership from the following:

a. Guiding [ ]

b. Influencing [ ]

c. Protecting [ ]

d. Loving [ ]

e. Controlling [ ]

2.2. Do you have any ideal leader (person) who influenced

you most for various reasons? Please mention from the following list.

a) Mother [ ]

b) Father [ ]

c) Teacher [ ]

d) Spouse [ ]

e) Friend [ ]

f) Uncle [ ]

g) Religious Guru [ ]

h) Politician [ ]

i) Boss(Supervisor) [ ]

3. Leadershop (Action)

3.1. What kind of benefits or qualities or skills you have derived from your leader?

A. Benefits

a. Power [ ]

b. Financial benefits [ ]

c. Employment [ ]

d. Promotion [ ]

e. Social status [ ]

f. Knowledge [ ]

g. Moral support [ ]

B. Qualities

a. Ambition [ ]

b. Courage [ ]

c. Perseverance [ ]
d. Self-confidence [ ]
e. Patience [ ]
f. Tolerance [ ]
g. Humility [ ]
h. Compassion [ ]
i. Discipline [ ]
j. Competitive spirit [ ]
k. Spirituality [ ]
l. Justice [ ]
m. Forgiveness [ ]
n. Kindness [ ]
o. Vision [ ]

C. Skills

a. The art of communication [ ]
b. The art of listening [ ]
c. The art of living [ ]
d. Administrative skills [ ]
e. Decision making skill [ ]
f. Tact and diplomacy [ ]
g. Inspirational power [ ]
h. Humour [ ]
i. Industry/Hard work [ ]

3.2. Do you consider that some of the following qualities are also essential to become a leader? Please tick.

a. Ego [ ]

b. Selfishness [ ]

c. Pride [ ]

d. Anger [ ]

e. Greed [ ]

f. Pomp [ ]

g. Envy [ ]

h. Harshness [ ]

i. Arrogance [ ]

j. Hypocrisy [ ]

k. Cunningness [ ]

3.3. Do you derecognise your superior for the reason of any one or a few qualities from the following list.

a. Timidity [ ]

b. Insincerity [ ]

c. Laziness [ ]

d. Ignorance [ ]

e. Pessimism [ ]

f. Indifference [ ]

SCHEDULE –III

Leadership Self-Perception

Below are given some statements regarding the behaviour of a leader. Please judge to what extent they are true or false for you when you are in the leadership role. Put a circle around one of the five responses against each statement.

QT – Quite True; T – True; D – Doubtful; F – False; QF – Quite False

1. I maintain partnership in the group. QT T D F QF
2. I help my subordinates in their career planning. QT T D F QF
3. I keep crucial information to myself. QT T D F QF
4. I help my subordinates to grow up and assume responsibility. QT T D F QF
5. I explain to my subordinates what I expect from them and what they can expect from me. QT T D F QF
6. I make my subordinates feel free even to disagree with me. QT T D F QF
7. I believe that top boss makes major decisions and implements them. QT T D F QF
8. I provide all information to my subordinates and let them jointly find the solution to a problem. QT T D F QF
9. I behave as if power and prestige are necessary for getting compliance from the subordinates. QT T D F QF
10. I help my subordinates even in their family matters. QT T D F QF
11. I interact with my subordinates as if they are equal. QT T D F QF
12. I maintain fair but impersonal relationship in the group. QT T D F QF
13. I go by the joint decisions of the group. QT T D F QF

14. I take special care to get the work done with top priority. QT T D F QF

15. I treat all group members as my equals. QT T D F QF

16. I believe that most of the interpersonal troubles start because people try to be over friendly and informal on the job. QT T D F QF

17. I maintain high standard of performance. QT T D F QF

18. I believe that subordinates acquire sense of responsibility under the care and guidance of a good leader. QT T D F QF

19. I think that if clear-cut job descriptions are available, there will be less conflicts in the organization. QT T D F QF

20. I expect my subordinates to increase their knowledge on the job. QT T D F QF

21. I believe that not all employees are capable of becoming officers. QT T D F QF

22. I openly show affection to those subordinates who work hard. QT T D F QF

23. I take the decision quickly and I am confident of being right. QT T D F QF

24. I give as much responsibility as my subordinates can handle. QT T D F QF

25. I believe that one can really grow up by learning to do a job well. QT T D F QF

26. I consider seniority as a time-tested criterion for promotion. QT T D F QF

27. I see that subordinates work to their capacity. QT T D F QF

28. I always follow rules and regulations. QT T D F QF

29. I grant full freedom and autonomy to my subordinates so that they can work hard. QT T D F QF

30. I rule with an iron hand to get the work done. QT T D F QF

31. I want to have full power and control over my subordinates. QT T D F QF

32. I create a climate where members respect each other's Individuality. QT T D F QF

33. I believe that all of us have more or less equal potentialities. QT T D F QF

34. I drive myself very hard. QT T D F QF

35. I categorise my subordinates as good and bad. QT T D F QF

36. I help the subordinates in their needs as much as I can. QT T D F QF

37. I give directions to my subordinates when it is necessary. QT T D F QF

38. I favour that the area of responsibility should be clearly demarcated according to rank and positions. QT T D F QF

39. I always keep track of the progress of the work. QT T D F QF

40. I confine myself to my own jurisdiction. QT T D F QF

41. I inform my subordinates how well they are doing their job. QT T D F QF

42. I feel responsible for the well being of my subordinates. QT T D F QF

43. I make it clear that personal loyalty is an important virtue. QT T D F QF

44. I am a friendly type. QT T D F QF

45. I never question the well established ways of doing things in the organization. QT T D F QF

46. I try to have strict division of labour even in my own group. QT T D F QF

47. I find time to listen to the personal problems of the subordinates. QT T D F QF

48. I do not tolerate any interference from my subordinates. QT T D F QF

49. I have affection for my subordinates. QT T D F QF

50. I believe that if I am not alert all the time there are many people who may pull me down. QT T D F QF

SCHEDULE-IV

Subodinates' Perception on Superior Styles

Below are given some statements regarding the behaviour of a leader. Please judge to what extent they are true or false. Put a circle around one of the five responses against each statement.

QT – Quite True; T – True; D – Doubtful; F – False; QF – Quite False

1. He maintains partnership in the group. QT T D F QF

2. He helps us in our career planning. QT T D F QF

3. He keeps crucial information to himself alone. QT T D F QF

4. He helps us to grow up and assume responsibility. QT T D F QF

5. He explains to us what he expect from us and what we can expect from him. QT T D F QF

6. He makes us feel free even to disagree with him. QT T D F QF

7. He believes that the top boss makes major decisions and implements them. QT T D F QF

8. He provides all information to us and let us jointly find the solution of a problem. QT T D F QF

9. He behaves as if power and prestige are necessary for getting compliance from us. QT T D F QF

10. He helps us even in our family matters. QT T D F QF

11. He interacts with us as if we are equal. QT T D F QF

12. He maintains fair but impersonal relationship in the group. QT T D F QF

13. He goes by the joint decisions of the group. QT T D F QF

14. He takes special care to get the work done with top priority. QT T D F QF

15. He treats all group members as his equals. QT T D F QF

16. He believes that most of the interpersonal troubles start because people try to be over friendly and informal on the job. QT T D F QF

17. He maintains high standard of performance. QT T D F QF

18. He believes that we acquire sense of responsibility under the care and guidance of a good leader. QT T D F QF

19. He thinks that if clear-cut job descriptions are available, there will be less conflicts in the organization. QT T D F QF

20. He expects from us to increase our knowledge on the job. QT T D F QF

21. He believes that not all employees are capable of becoming officers. QT T D F QF

22. He openly shows affection to those subordinates who work hard. QT T D F QF

23. He takes the decision quickly and he is confident of being right. QT T D F QF

24. He gives as much responsibility as we can handle. QT T D F QF

25. He believes that one can really grow up by learning to do a job well. QT T D F QF

26. He considers seniority as a time-tested criterion for promotion. QT T D F QF

27. He sees that we work to our capacity. QT T D F QF

28. He always follows rules and regulations. QT T D F QF

29. He grants full freedom and autonomy to us so that we can work hard. QT T D F QF

30. He rules with an iron hand to get the work done. QT T D F QF

31. He wants to have full power and control over us. QT T D F QF

32. He creates a climate where members respect each other's individuality. QT T D F QF

33. He believes that all of us have more or less equal potentialities. QT T D F QF

34. He drives himself very hard. QT T D F QF

35. He categorises us as good and bad. QT T D F QF

36. He helps us in need as much as he can. QT T D F QF

37. He gives directions to us when it is necessary. QT T D F QF

38. He favours that the area of responsibility should be clearly demarcated according to rank and positions. QT T D F QF

39. He always keeps track of the progress of the work. QT T D F QF

40. He confines himself to his own jurisdiction. QT T D F QF

41. He informs us how well we are doing our job. QT T D F QF

42. He feels responsible for the well being of us. QT T D F QF

43. He makes it clear that personal loyalty is an important virtue. QT T D F QF

44. He is a friendly type. QT T D F QF
45. He never questions the well established ways of doing things in the organization. QT T D F QF
46. He tries to have strict division of labour even in his own group. QT T D F QF
47. He finds time to listen to our personal problems. QT T D F QF
48. He does not tolerate any interference from us. QT T D F QF
49. He has affection for us. QT T D F QF
50. He believes that if he is not alert all the time there are many people who may pull him down. QT T D F QF

Bibliography

Amin, D.L. "Perception of the First Line Supervisor about His Job," *Industrial Relations*, IIBM, Calcutta, 1963.

Anderson, L.R. "Some Effects of Leadership Training on Intercultural Discussion Groups," University of Illinois, Group Effectiveness Research Laboratory, Technical Report, Urbana, (1964).

Ansari, M.A. "Need for Nurturant-Task Leaders in India: Some empirical evidence," *Management and Labour Studies*, 11,1, (1986).

Apple White, Phillip B., *Organisational Behaviour*, Englewood Cliffs, Prentice-Hall, New Jersey, 1965 (Chapter 6).

Argyris C. Schon D. *Theory in Practice*, Jossy - Bass, San-Francisco, California, 1974.

Argyris, C. "Theories in Action that Inhibit Individual Leaving", *American Psychologist*, Vol.31, 1976.

B.J. Hodge and Johnson H.J., *Management of Organisational Behaviour*, John Wiley and Sons, New York, 1970.

B.L. Jaggi, "Management Leadership Styles in Indian Work Organizations," *Indian Manager*, April-June 1978.

Bales, R.F. *Interaction Process Analysis: A Method for the study of Small Groups*, Cambridge, 1950.

Bass, B. M., *Leadership, Psychology and Organizational Behaviour*, Harper, New York, 1960.

Bass, B.M., *Leadership and Performance Beyond Expectations*, The Free Press, New York, 1985.

Baumgartel, H. "Leadership, Motivations and Attitudes in Research Laboratories," *Journal of Social Issues*, 12, (1956).

Bayati, J.L. "An Investigation into the Leader Behavior Characteristics of Higher Secondary School Pupils," *Journal of College Education*, Karnataka University, Dharwar, 6 (1969).

Bennis, W.G. "Leadership Theory and Administrative Behaviour: The Problem of Authority," *Administrative Science Quarterly*, Vol.4, 1959.

Bennis, W.G. "Leadership Theory and Administrative Behaviour: The Problem of Authority," *Administrative Science Quarterly*, 4, 1959.

Berkowitz, L. "An Exploratory Study of the Roles of Aircraft Commanders," USAF *Human Resource Research Center, Research Bulletin*, 56-65 (1953).

Bernard M. Bass, "Evolving Perspectives on Charismatic Leadership", in Jay A. Conger, Rabindra N. Kanungo, et al. (ed.) *Charismatic Leaders*,(Jossey-Bass, San Francisco, 1988).

Bernard M. Bass, "From Transactional to Transformational Leadership: Learning to Share the Vision," *Organizational Dynamics*, Winter 1990.

Bernard M. Bass, cited in Kenneth E. Clark and Miriam B. Clark (eds.), *Measures of Leadership*, A center for Creative Leadership Book, Leadership Library of America, West Orange, New Jersey, 1990.

Bhatt, L. J. and Pathak, N.S. "A Study of Functions of Supervisory Staff and Characteristics Essential for Success as viewed by a Group of Supervisors," *Manas*, 9 (1962).

Bhusan, L.I. "Leadership Performance as related to Age, Education, Residence and Sex," *Indian Journal of Social Work*, July, Volume 1, (1968).

Blake, R.R. and Mouton, S.J., *The Managerial Grid*, Gulf Publishing Company, Houston, Taxaus, 1964.

Bogardus, E.S., *Essentials of Social Psychology*, University of Southern California Press, Los Angels, 1918.

Brunson, R.W. and Wickhert, F.R. "The Empirical Investigation at the Contingency Theory within a Conglomerate," Paper Presented at the American Psychological Association, 1973.

Byrd, C., *Social Psychology*, Appleton – Century – Crofts, 1940.

C.A. Myer, *Industrial Relations in India*, Asia Publishing House, Bombay, 1960.

Calvin, A.D., Hoffmann, F.K. and Harden, E.L. "The Effect of Intelligence and Social Atmosphere on Group Problem Solving Behavior," *Journal of Social Psychology*, 45, (1957).

Campbell, D.P. *Campbell Leadership Index Manual*, National Computer System, 1991.

Carter, L.F. "Leadership and Small Group Behaviour," in M. Sheriff and M.O. Wilson, eds., *Group Relations at the Crossroads*, Harper, 1953.

Cattell, R.B. and Stice, G.F. "Four formulae for Selecting Leaders on the basis of Personality," *Human Relations*, 7 (1954).

Charles C. Manz and Henry P. Sims, Jr., "Super Leadership: Beyond the Myth of Heroic Leadership", *Organizational Dynamics*, Spring 1991.

Chatterjee, A. "Satisfaction and Productivity: A Study of Morale and Team Work in Industry with Respect of Productivity," I.I.S. Ph.D. Thesis, Bangalore, 1961.

Chester I Barnard, *The Functions of the Executive*, Harvard University Press, Cambridge, 1946.

Chowdhry, K. "An analysis of the Attitudes of Textile Workers and the Effects of those Attitudes on Work Efficiency," *Human Relation Division Research Note.*, ATIRA, 3 (1953).

Chris Argyris, *Executive Leadership*, Harper and Brothers Publishers, New York, 1953.

Conger, Jam. and Kanungo, R. "Toward A Behavioural Theory of Charismatic Leadership in Organizational Setting," *Academy of Management Review*, Vol.12, No.4, October 1987.

Conger, The Charismatic Leader; Jane M. Howell and Bruce Avolio, "The Ethics of Charismatic Leadership: Submission or Liberation?" *The Executive*, May 1992.

Conway, M., *The Crown in Peace and War*, Long-mans Green, New York, 1915.

Daniel Katz et al. *Productivity, Supervision and Morale in Office Situation*, Survey Research Centre, University of Michigan, Ann Arbor, 1950.

David A. Whetten and Kim S. Cameron, *Developing Management Skills*, Harper Collins, New York, 1991.

Davis Kipnis, Stuart M. Schmidt, Chris Swaffin-Smith, and Ian Wilkinson, "Pattern of Managerial Influence: Shotgun Managers, Tacicians, and By Standards," *Organisational Dynamics*, Winter 1984.

Douglas McGregor., *The Human Side of Enterprise*, McGraw-Hill International Book Company, New York, 1960.

Elhance, D.N. and Agarwal, R.D. "Delegation of Authority," *Lok Udyog*, 6 (1973).

Evans, M.G. "The Effect of Supervisory Behaviour on the Path-Goal Relationship," *Organizational Behaviour and Human Performance*, 5 (1970).

Fiedler, F.E., "A Contingency Model of Leadership Effectiveness," Berkowitz (Ed.), Advances in Experimental Social Psychology, Academic Press, New York, 1964.

Fiedler, F.E. "Style or Circumstance: The Leadership Enigma", *Psychology Today*, March, 1969.

Fiedler, F.E., *A Theory of Leadership Effectiveness*, McGraw Hill, New York, 1967.

Filley, A.C., House, R.J. and Kerr, S., *Managerial Process and Organizational Behaviour*, 2nd Ed. Scott, Foresman, 1976.

Fleishman, E.A. "Leadership Climate, Human Relations Training, and Supervisory Behaviour," *Personnel Psychology*, Vol.6, No.2, Summer, 1953.

Fleishman, E.A. and Simmons, J. "Relationship between Leadership Patterns and Effectiveness ratings among Israeli foreman," *Personnel Psychology*, 23 (1970).

Fox, W.M. "Group Reaction to two types of Conference Leadership," *Human Relations*, 10, 1957.

Fred Luthans, "Leadership: A Proposal for a Social Learning Theory Base and Observational and Functional Analysis Techniques to Measure Leader Behaviour," in J.G. Hunt And L.L. Larson (Eds.), *Crosscurrents in Leadership*, Southern Illinois University Press, Carbondale and Edwardsville, Illinois, 1979.

Ganguli, H.C., *Structure and Process of Organisation*, Asia Publishing House, Bombay, 1964.

Gary A. Yukl, *Leadership in Organisations*, 2nd ed. Prentice Hall, Englewood Cliffs, New Jersey, 1989.

George R. Terry, *Principles of Management*, Richard D. Irwin, Inc. Home Wood, Illinois, 1968.

George, F. Farris and Francis, G. Lim, Jr. "Effects of Performance on Leadership, Cohesiveness, Satisfaction and Subsequent Performance," *Journal of Applied Psychology*, Vol.53, No.6, December 1969.

Getzels, J.S. and Guba E.G. "Social Behaviour and the Administrative Process," *School Review*, 55 (1957).

Gheselli, E.E. "Management Talent", *American Psychologist*, Vol.18, Oct, 1963.

Gibb, C.A. "Leadership," in G. Lindzey and others., *Handbook of Social Psychology*, Addison-Wesley, Mass, 1954.

Gibb, C.A. "Leadership" in Lindzey, G. and Aronson, (Eds.) *Hand Book of Social Psychology*, Vol.4, Addison-Wesley, Mass, 1969.

Ginnett, R.C. "Team Effectiveness Leadership Model: Identifying Leverage Points for Change," Proceedings of the National Leadership Institute Conference, College Park, MD: National Leadership Institute, 1996.

Gore, W.J. and Silander, F.S. "A Bibliographical Essay on Decision Making," *Administrative Science Quarterly*, Vol.6, 1959.

Govindarajan, T.N. "A Study of Juvenile Delinquents Position in the Family," *Indian Journal of Applied Psychology*, 3 (1964).

Graham, W.K. "Leader Behavior, Esteem for Least-Preferred

Co-Worker, and Group Performance," American Psychological Association, 1968.

H.K. Kalra "Leadership Styles of Executives in Indian Enterprises," unpublished Research Report, Punjab Agricultural University, Ludhiana, 1980.

Habibullah, A.H.M. and Sinha, J.B.P. "Motivational Climate and Leadership Styles," *Vikalpa*, 5 (1980).

Haiman, F.S., *Group Leadership and Democratic Action*, Houghton Mifflin, Boston, 1951.

Harding, L. W. "Twenty-One Varieties of Educational Leadership," *Educational Leadership,* 6 (1949).

Hare, A.P. Borgatta, E.E., and Bales, R.F., *Small Groups Studies in Social Group Interaction*, New York, 1955.

Harold Koontz and Cyril O' Donnell, *Essentials of Management*, Tata McGraw-Hill Publishing Company, New Delhi, 1978.

Harold Koontz and Heinz Weihrich, *Essentials of Management*, 5th Edition, McGraw Hill Series in Management, New York, 1990.

Harris, E.F. and Fleishman, E.A. "Human Relations Training and the Stability of Leadership Patterns," *Journal of Applied Psychology*, 39 (1955).

Hemphill, J.K. "The Leader and his Group," *Journal of Educational Research*, 28 (1949).

Henry Fayol, *General and Industrial Management*, Pitman and Sons, London, 1949.

Henry Mintzberg, *The Nature of Managerial Work*, Harper and Row, New York, 1973; J. Kenneth Graham, Jr., and William L. Mihal, "The CMD Managerial Job Analysis Inventory," Rochester Institute of Technology, Center for Management Development, Rochester, New York, 1987.

Henry Mintzberg, *The Nature of Managerial work*, Prentice Hall, Englewood Cliffs, New Jersey, 1980.

Herbert G. Hicks and C. Roy Gullet, *The Management of Organizations*, 3rd edition, McGraw-Hill Series in Management, New York.

Hingar, Asha, *Leadership Styles and Job Satisfaction*, Printwell Publishers, Jaipur, 1986.

Hollander, E.P., and Jullian J.W., "Contemporary Trends in the Analysis of Leadership Processes," *Psychological Bulletin*, 71, 1996.

House, R.J. "A Path-Goal Theory of Leadership Effectiveness", *Administrative Science Quarterly*, Vol.16, Sep.1971.

House, R.J. and Dessler G. "The Path-Goal Theory of Leadership", in Hunt J.G. and Larson, L. (Eds) *Contingency Approaches to Leadership*, Souther Illionois, University Press, 1974.

Hunt, J.W., *Managing People at Work*, Second Edition, McGraw-Hill, New York, 1986.

Ivancevich, Donnelly and Gibson, *Management Principles and Functions*, Fourth edition, All India Traveller Book seller, Delhi, 1991.

Ivancevich, Szilagyi and Wallace, *Organisation Behaviour and Performance*, p.273 (Adopted from Dr. M.J. Mathew, "Organisation: Theory and Behaviour," RBSA Publishers, Jaipur, 1993, p.181)

J. M. Burns, *Leadership*, Harper and Row, New York, 1978.

Jain, U. "Life Styles of Indian Managers: An Exploratory Study of the Images, Experiences and Impact of Collectors in their Districts," Unpublished Fellow Programme Dissertation, Indian Institute of Management, Ahmedabad, India, 1982.

James J. Cribbin, *Effective Managerial Leadership*, American Management Association, 1972.

James M. Kouzes and Barry Z. Posner, *The Leadership Challenge: How to Get Extraordinary Things Done in Organizations*, Jossey-Bass, San Francisco, 1987.

James Owen, "The Uses of Leadership Theory", *Michigan Business Review*, Vol.25, No.1, January, 1973.

Jennings, E.E. "The Anatomy of Leadership", *Management of Personnel Quarterly*, Vol.1, Autumn, 1961.

John P. Kotter, *A Force for Change: How Leadership Differs from Management*, The Free Press, New York, 1990;

John R.P. French and Betram Raven, "The Basis of Social Power," in *Studies in Social Power*. D. Cart Wright, University of Michigan Press, Ann Arbor, 1959.

Joseph Reitz, H. "Behaviour in Organizations," Rev. Ed. (Home Wood III. Irwin, 1981) and Paul Heresy and Kenneth H. Blanchard, *Management of Organizational Behaviour*, 3rd Ed. Englewood Cliffs, Prentice- Hall, N.J., 1977.

Kakabadse, Andrew, "Leadership for the Third Millennium," *Essence of Leadership*, International Thompson Publishing, 1998.

Kakar, S., *Personality and Authority in Work*, Somaiya Publications, Bombay, 1974.

Kapila, P.D. 'Leadership Styles in Public Sector', in Narayan, B. (Ed) *Leadership and Managerial Effectiveness,* Janaki Prakashan, New Delhi, 1987.

Karmel, B. "Leadership: A Challenge to Traditional Research Methods and Assumptions," *Academy of Management Review*, Vol.3, 1978.

Katz. D.N., Maccoby and Morse, N. "Productivity, Supervision, and Morale in an Office Situation," Survey Research Center, Institute for Social Research, University of Michigan, Ann Arber, Michigan, 1950.

Katzell, R.A., Miller, C.E., Rotter, N.G., and Vinet, T.G. "Effects of Leadership and other Inputs on Group Processes and Outputs," *Journal of Social Psychology*, 80, (1970).

Keith Davis, *Human Behaviour at Work*, Tata McGraw-Hill Company Ltd., New Delhi, 1975.

Khan, R. and Katz D. "Leadership Practices in Relation to Productivity and Morale" in *Group Dynamics, Research and Theory*, 2nd Ed. D. Cartwright and A. Zander Elonsford, Row, Paterson, New York, 1960.

Kidd, J.S., and Christy, R.T. "Supervisory Procedures and Work Team Productivity," *Journal of Applied Psychology*, 45, (1961).

Koontz O' Donnell, *Management*, McGraw-Hill International Book Company, 1st Printing, New York, 1984.

Koontz, H. and O' Donnel, C., *Management*, McGraw-Hill, New York, 1976.

Koontz, H. and Weihrich, H., *Management*, 9th Edition, McGraw-Hill Company, Yew York, 1989.

Korman, A.K. "Consideration, Initiating Structure and Organizational Criteria: A Review," *Personnel Psychology*, 19 (1966).

Krech, D., Crutchfield, R.S. and Ballachey, E.L., *Individual in Society*, McGraw-Hill, New York, 1962.

Krech, E. and Crutchfield, R.S., *Theory and Problems of Social Psychology*, McGraw Hill, New York, 1948.

Kumar, Usha and Singh, K.K. "The Inter-Personal Construct System of the Indian Manager: A determinant of Organizational Behaviour," *Indian Journal of Psychology*, 51 (1976), 275-278, (p.288).

Kunhert, K.W. and Lewis, P. "Transactional and Transformational Leadership: A Constructive and A developmental Analysis," *Academy of Management Review*, Vol.12, No.4, 1987.

Lanzetta, J.T. and Roby, T.B. "The Relationship Between Certain Group Process Variables and Group Problem Solving Efficiency," *Journal of Social Psychology*, 52, (1960).

Levine, S. "An Approach to Constructive Leadership," *Journal of Sociological Issues*, 5 (1949).

Lewin, K., Lippitt, R. and White, R.K. "Patterns of Aggressive Behaviour in Experimentally Created 'Social Climates'", *Journal of Social Psychology*, Vol.10, 1939.

Lewin, Lippitt, R., and White, R.K. "Patterns of Aggressive Behaviour in Experimentally Created 'Social Climates'," *Journal of Psychology*, 1939.

Lokhande M.R. and Singh S.N. "Leadership Patterns and Social Change," *Journal of the Council of Social Development*, Volume 7, No.1, March 1977.

Lynn R. Anderson, "Towards a Two-Track Model of Leadership Training: Suggestions from Self-Monitoring Theory," *Small Group Research*, Vol.21, No.2, May 1990.

Maier, N.F.R. "The Quality of Group Decisions as Influenced by the Discussion Leader," *Human Relations*, 6, (1950).

Manisha Agarwal and G.C. Agarwal "Relationship of Middle Managers' Power Styles with their Participativeness at the Work Place," *Indian Journal of Industrial Relations*, Volume 30, No.3, January 1995.

Max Weber, cited in S.N. Eisenstadt, *Max Weber: On Charisma and Institution Building*," University of Chicago Press, Chicago, 1968.

McCurely, H.G., and Eber, H.W. "Democratic Versus Authoritarian: A Further Investigation of Group Problem Solving," *Journal of Personality*, 22, (1953).

McGregor, D., *The Human Side of Enterprise*, McGraw-Hill, New York, 1960.

Merton, R.K. "The Social Nature of Leadership," *American Journal of Nursing*, 69, 1969.

Meuwese, W.A.T. and Fiedler, F.E. "Leadership and Group Creativity under varying conditions of Stress," University of Illinois, Group Effectiveness Research Laboratory, Technical Report, Urbana 1965.

Michael J. Marquart and Dean W. Engel, "HRD Competencies for a Shrinking World," *Training and Development*, May 1993.

Misumi, J., *The Validation of Conceptional Model of Leadership Partners*, Institute of Group Dynamics, Kyushu University, Japan, 1972.

Morris, W.T. and Seeman, M. "The Problem of Leadership: An Interdisciplinary Approach," *American Journal of Sociology*, 56 (1950).

Mullen, J.H. "Differential Leadership Modes and Productivity in a Large Organization," *Academy of Management Journal*, 3 (1965).

Munson, C.E. "Style and Structure in Supervision", *Journal of Education for Social Work*, 17, 1981.

Muttayya, B.C. and Vijaya Kumar, S. "Leadership Styles, Perceived Need Satisfaction and Subjective Job Characteristics among Scientific Personnel," *Indian*

Journal of Industrial Relations, Volume-21; No.2, October 1985.

N. Panchanatham, K. Rajendran, and K. K. Karuppiah "A Study of Executive Leadership Styles and problem Solving Behaviour," *Indian Journal of Industrial Relations*, Volume-29, No.1, July 1993.

Nanus. B., *Visionary Leadership*, Free Press, New York, 1992.

Neelam Varma, "A Test of Implicit Personality Theories of Leadership," *Indian Journal of Industrial Relations*, Volume 22, No.2, Oct, 1986.

Nitish De, "Dilemmas of Indian Managers," *Management in Government*, July-September 1974.

Noel M. Tichy and Mary Anne Devanna, "The Transformational Leader," *Training and Development Journal*, July 1986.

Omer Bin Sayeed "Conflict Management Styles: Relationship with Leadership Styles and Moderating Effect of Esteem for Coworker," *Indian Journal of Industrial Relations*, Vol.26, No.1, July 1990.

Ordway Tead, *The Art of Leadership*, McGraw Hill Book Company, Inc. New York, 1953.

Ouchi, W.G., *Theory Z: How American Business can meet the Japanese Challenge*, Addison-Wesley, 1981.

P.M. Joseph and R.Kesavan, "A Comparative Study of Leader Behaviour in Public and Private Sectors in India," *Indian Manager*, April-June 1977.

Paul Hersey and K.H. Blanchard, *Management of Organisational Behaviour*, Engle wood Cliffs, Prentice Hall, New Jersey, 1977.

Paul Hersey and Kenneth H. Blanchard, *Management of Organisational Behaviour*, Engle Wood Cliffs, Prentice Hall, New Jersey, 1979.

Peter Drucker, *Practice of Management*, Allied publishers, New Delhi, 1970.

Pigors, P. "Types of Leaders in Group Work," *Sociology and Social.Research*, 21 (1936).

Prabhakar Singh "Nurturant Task and Participative Task Leaderships: The Effective Leader Behaviours for Indian Industries," *Indian Journal of Industrial Relations*, Volume.23, No.2, October 1987.

R. Venkatapathy "Perception of Top Management Leadership Styles and Climate: A Study of Public and Private Executives," *Indian Journal of Industrial Relations*, Volume-25, No.3, January 1990.

R.J. House, "A Path-Goal Theory of Leader Effectiveness," *Administrative Science Quarterly*, September 1971, pp.321-338, and R.J. House and T.R.Mitchel, "Path-Goal Theory of Leadership," *Journal of Contemporary Business*, Autumn, 1974.

R.P. Singh and Janak Pandey "Leadership Styles, Control Strategies and Personal Consequences," *Indian Journal of Industrial Relations*, Volume 22, No.1, July 1986.

R.Rangaswamy and D.Helmick, "A Comparative Study of Indian and American Executives' Leadership Styles," *Indian Administrative and Management Review*, July-September 1976.

Rabindra M. Kanungo and Sasi Misra, "Managerial Resourcefulness: A Reconceptualization of Management Skills," *Human Relations*, December 1992.

Rajinder Kaur, "Managerial Styles in the Public Sector," *Indian Journal of Industrial Relations*, Volume 28, No.4, April, 1993.

Ralph M. Stogdill, "Personal Factors Associated with

Leadership: A Survey of the Literature", *Journal of Psychology*, Jan.1948.

Ralph M. Stogdill, *Handbook of Leadership: A Survey of Theory and Research*, The Free Press, New York, 1974.

Rama J. Joshi "Managerial Effectiveness: As Perceived by Chief Executives," *Indian Journal of Industrial Relations*, Volume 27, No.1, July 1991.

Rama Murthy, R. "Study on Leadership Styles in State Owned Enterprises," *Journal of General Management*, Volume 2, Winter, 1987.

Ramakanth. J. "Attitudes of Managers in Public Enterprises," unpublished Thesis Submitted to Osmania University, Hyderabad, 1985.

Rambo, W.W. "The Construction and analysis of a Leadership Behavior Rating Form," *Journal of Applied Psychology*, 42 (1958).

Reddin J. William. "The 3-D Management Style Theory," *Training and Development Journal*, April 1967.

Rensis Likert, *New Pattern of Management*, McGraw-Hill, New York, 1961.

Rensis Likert, *The Human Organization*, McGraw Hill, New York, 1967.

Roach, C.F. and Behling, O. "Functionalism: Basis for an Alternative Approach to the Study of Leadership," in *Leadership and Managers* by J.G. Hunt (ed.), Pergamon, New York, 1984.

Robbins, S.P., *Organisational Behaviour: Concepts and Controversies*, Engle wood cliffs, Prentice Hall, New Jersey, 1979.

Robert J. House,"A 1976 Theory of Charismatic Leadership," in J. G. Hunt And L. L. Larson (eds), *Leadership: The*

Cutting Edge Southern Illinois University Press, Carbondale, 1977.

Robert L. Katz, "The Skills of an Effective Administrator," *Harvard Business Review*, September-October 1974.

Robert R. Blake and Jane S. Mouton., *The Managerial Grid,* (Gulf Publishing, Houston, 1978) Kurt Lewin, Ronald Lippitt and Ralph K. White "Patterns of Aggressive Behaviour in Experimentally Created Social Climates", *Journal of Social Psychology*, Vol.10, No.2, May, 1939.

Robert Tannenbaum and Warren H. Schmidt, "How to choose a Leadership Pattern," *Harvard Business Review* (March – April 1958), pp.95-101, and Heinz Weihrich, "How to Change a Leadership pattern," *Management Review* (April 1979).

Robert Tannenbaum, R. Weschier and Fred Massarik, *Leadership and Organisation: A Behavioural Science approach*, McGraw-Hill Book Co., Inc., New York, 1961.

S. Selvadurai, "Leadership in the Co-operatives: Some perceptions of Leaders," *Indian management*, July 1997.

S.D. Punekar and M.G.Savur, *Management - White Collar Relations,* Popular Prakashan, Bombay, 1969.

S.P. Robbins, *Organisational Behaviour*, Prentice Hall Inc., Englewood Cliffs, 1979.

Sadler, P.J. "Leadership Style, Confidence in Management, and Job Satisfaction," *Journal of Applied Behavioural Science*, 6 (1970).

Sanderson, D. and Nafe, R.W. "Studies in Rural Leadership," Publ. Amer. Social. Soc., 23 (1929).

Schuler, R.S. "Role Perception, Satisfaction and Performance Moderated by Organization Level and Participation in Decision-Making," *Academy of Management Journal*, 20, (1977).

Sequeria, C.E. "Functions of a Supervisor," *Indian Journal of Applied Psychology*, 1, (1962).

Shartle, C.L. "Studies in Naval Leadership," in H. Guetzkow Groups, *Leadership and Men*, Carnegie Press, Pittsburgh, 1951.

Shaw, M.E. "A Comparison of two types of Leadership in Various Communication Nets," *Journal of Abnormal and Social Psychology*, 50, (1955).

Shaw, M.E., and Blum, J.M. "Effects of Leadership Style upon Group Performance as a Function of Task Structure," *Journal of Personality and Social Psychology*, 1966.

Siegel, J. P. "A Study of the Relationship among Organizational Factors, Personality Traits, Job and Leadership Attitudes," *Dissertation Abstracts*, 29 (1969).

Singh, A.P. and Das, G.S. "Management Style of Indian Manager: A profile," ASCI *Journal of Management*, September 1977.

Singh, P. "Leadership Process and its Impact on Productivity, Satisfaction and Work Commitment," *Decision*, Volume 6, 1979.

Sinha J.B.P. "The Authoritative Leadership: A Style of Effective Management," *Indian Journal of Industrial Relations*, 11 (1976).

Sinha, J.B.P. and Chowdary, G.P. "Perception of Subordinates as a Moderator of Leadership Effectiveness," A.N.S. Institute of Social Studies, Patna, 1979(mimeographed).

Sinha, J.B.P., *The Nurturant Task-Behaviour*, Concept Publishing Company, New Delhi, 1980.

Sinha, T.N. and Sinha, J.B.P. "Styles of Leadership and their effects on Group Productivity," A.N.S. Institute of Social Studies, Patna, 1977 (mimeographed).

Sinha. D. and Kumar P. "A Study of Certain Personality Variables in Student Leadership," *Psychological Studies*, 11 (1966).

Skinner, Elizabeth, W. "Relationships between Leadership Behaviour Patterns and Organizational Situational Variables," *Personnel Psychology*, 22 (1969).

Spector, P. and Suttell Barbara, J. "Research on the specific leader behaviour patterns most effective in influencing group performance," American Institute for Research, Washington, D.C., 1956.

Steven Kerr and John M. Jermier, "Substitutes for Leadership: Their Meaning and Measurement", *Organisational Behaviour and Human Performance*, December 1978.

Steven Kerr, Chester, A. Schniesheim, Charles J. Murphy, and Ralph. M. Stogdill. "Toward a Contingency Theory of Leadership based upon the Consideration and Initiating Structure Literature", *Organizational Behaviour and Human Performance*, August 1974.

Stogdill, R.M and Coons, A.E. (eds) "Leader Behaviour its Perception and Measurement," Columbus, Bureau of Business Research, Ohio State University, 1957.

Stogdill, R.M. "Managers, Employees, Organisations," Bureau of Business Research, Ohio State University, Columbus, 1965.

Stogdill, R.M. "Personal Factors Associated with Leadership: A Survey of Literature", *Journal of Psychology*, Vol.25, 1948.

Stogdill, R.M. and Coons, A.E. (Ed) "Leader Behaviour: Its Description and Measurement," Research Monograph No.88, Bureau of Business Research, Ohio State University, Columbus, 1957.

Stogdill, R.M., *Hand Book of Leadership: A Survey of Theory and Research*, Free Press, New York, 1974.

Stogdill, R.M., *Individual Behaviour and Group Achievement*, Oxford University Press, New York, 1959.

Subramanian and K. Sajjan Rao "Attitudes of Union Leaders in Changing Realities- Direction Towards Greater Involvement," *Indian Journal of Industrial Relations*, Volume 32, No.4, April 1997.

Swarna Pratap and Srivastava, S.K. "Leadership Styles and Effectiveness: A comparative study," *Indian Journal of Industrial Relations*, Volume 21, No.1, July 1985.

Syed Vazith Hussain "Leadership Styles in Small Scale Industries," *The Indian Journal of Commerce*, Vol.55, No.3, July-September 2002.

Szilagyi and Wallace, "Organisational Behaviour and Performance," Richard D. Irwin, Inc. Homewood, Illinois, 1968.

Tannenbaum, R. and Schmidt, W.H. "How to Choose a Leadership Pattern," *Harvard Business Review*, May-June, 1973.

Thiagarajan, K.M. and Deep, S.D. "A Study of Supervisor Subordinate Influence on Satisfaction in four Cultures," *Journal of Social Psychology*, 82 (1970).

Tichy, N.M. and Devanna, M.A., *The Transformational Leader*, Wiley, New York, 1986.

Tosi, H. "A Re-Examination of Personality as a determinant of the effects of Participation," *Personnel Psychology*, 23 (1970).

V. Ravichandran and D. Nagabrahmam "Leadership in a Transitory Environment," *Indian Journal of Industrial Relations*, Volume 32, No.4, April 1997.

V.H. Vroom and P.W. Yetton, *Leadership and Decision-Making*, University of Pittsburgh Press, Pittsburgh, 1973.

V.S.P. Rao and P.S. Narayana, *Organisation Theory and Behaviour*, Vikas Publishing House, New Delhi, 1986.

Verma, Jyoti. "A scale for measuring Leadership styles," A.N.S. Institute of social studies, Patna, 1977 (mimeographed).

Vroom V.H. and Yetton P.W., *Leadership and Decision Making*, University of Pittsburgh Press, 1973.

Vroom, V. and Mann, F. "Leader Authoritarianism and Employee Attitudes," *Personnel Psychology*, 13 (1960).

Vroom, V., *Some Personality Determinants of the Effects of Participation*, Prentice Hall, Englewood Cliffs, N.J., 1960.

Vroom, V.H., *The Search for a Theory of Leadership in Contemporary Management: Issues and View Points*, Ed. Joseph W. McGuire, Englewood Cliffs, N.J., Prentice-Hall, 1974.

W.J. Reddin, *Managerial Effectiveness*, McGraw-Hill, New York, 1970.

Weschler, J.R., Kahane, M., and Tannenbaum, R. "Job Satisfaction, Productivity, and Morale: A Case Study," *Occupational Psychology*,26, (1952).

Wexley, K.N., Singh, J.P. and Yukl, G.A. "Subordinate Personality as Moderator of the Effects of Participation in three types of Appraisal Interviews," *Journal of Applied Psychology*, 58 (1973).

Yukl, G.A. "Leader Personality and Situational Variables as Co-Determinants of Leader Behavior," *Dissertation Abstract*, 29 (1968).

Yukl, Gary., *Leadership in Organizations*, Prentice Hall, Englewood Cliffs, New Jersey, 1981.

Index

■■■